I0164236

My name is Freddie and I will be your host during your journey through our booklet.

September 2017

STORY TELLING

FOUR

MAGAZINE

STORY TELLING SERIES IS PUBLISHED QUARTERLY

A compilation of short stories, yarns, rhymes and blogs.

SOME ARE LONG
AND SOME ARE TRUE
THERE ARE ONES
THAT ARE SHORT
AND OTHERS ARE BLUE
ALL ARE THOUGHT PROVOKING
WITH FUNNY ONES WORTH A
GIGGLE OR TWO

STORY TELLING FOUR

MAGAZINE
PUBLISHED QUARTERLY

ISBN 978 0 9956917 3 5

Published by

Percychatteybooks Publisher

© Percy W Chattey 2017

As always for my lovely wife Jean, friend and soul mate, who has helped with the editing and all rewrites, also listening to all my ramblings whilst putting these articles together.

My appreciation to the following
Derek Cook for the cover
Christopher Wyatt
Richard Seal
Trudie Le Beau
Pete Broadbent
Tony Wilson
Dan Lake
Tim O'Rourke
Phil Lawler
Ray Enos
Lee Trevino
Stuart Fisk
All my friends on Social Media who send me their gems.

The Story Telling Series is looking for short stories, anecdotes for inclusion in our next issue, please send to percybooks@outlook.com *all entries will be acknowledged.*

But First let me explain the following as it is very important:

The contents and the opinion shown or written here are not necessarily the views of 'Story Telling' or its publisher and are published as articles of interest and amusement only and no offence of any kind religious, race or political is intended to any group of people.

~~~~~~~~~~~~~~~~~~~~~~~~~~~~~~~~~~~~~

OTHER BOOKS IN THIS SERIES
STORY TELLING
STORY TELLING TWO
STORY TELLING THREE

STORY TELLING FIVE WILL BE OUT IN DECEMBER

STORY TELLING FOUR

It is one hundred years since the bloody battle of Passchendaele and we start this issue by repeating Dan Lake's ditty detailing the horror and the dreadfulness of that period in the history of Europe.

On these fields of Passchendaele, skylarks sing and cattle graze; in these fields of Flanders lives were spent in far off days. No hint of what went on here! No sign of blood and bones; but sixty thousand souls rest here beneath the white headstones; on these fields of Passchendaele, where roam the silent sheep, the only sound the wailing winds; those mothers who still weep: Over fields of Passchendaele.....

On these fields of Passchendaele, men walked against the fire, while lead and splinters fell like rain, they clung to bloodied wire.

They prayed to God almighty that this day they might get through, but Gods not listening Tommy son, he hasn't time for you on these fields of Passchendaele; where donkey's planned their war. Far from the filthy trenches they were spared what lion's saw
on these fields of Passchendaele...

On these fields of Passchendaele I stand without a clue of what you poor men suffered, or what you had to do.
But I can feel your pain as a vice surrounds my heart, that crushes breath within me till it forces tears to start
for men who died so bloodily, from gas or lead and shell, who drowned in blood and mud, in this place of utter hell:
On these fields of Passchendaele....
By Dan Lake

LIVE ON

The Royal British Legion

The Legion, a World Wide Organisation was formed on the 15th May 1921 to bring aide to the injured ex-servicemen and their families, acquired during the horror of the Great War 1914 -1918.

The Legion is a Charity and has continued with this huge work through subsequent conflicts and does so to this day, spending one point five million pounds daily in support of those in need. Every year in recognition of Armistice Day, when fighting came to an end in November 1918, The Royal British Legion holds a service at the Royal Albert Hall in London, and in remembering the fallen in all wars, two minutes silence is held.

The Poppy appeal starts in October of each year, when collection tins are distributed in bars, shops and elsewhere, and we at 'Story Telling' ask that you support this wonderful organization to be able to continue in their task

This must have been some truckers nightmare!!!

Stress *You pick up a hitchhiker... A beautiful girl.*

Suddenly, she faints inside your truck and you take her to the hospital. Now that's stressful.

But at the hospital, they say she is pregnant and congratulate you that you're going to be a father. You say that you are not the father, but the girl says you are. This is getting very stressful!

You request a DNA test to prove that you are not the father. After the tests are completed, The doctor says the test shows you're infertile, And probably have been since birth. You're extremely stressed but relieved

On your way back home, you think about your 5 kids that are there. Now that is **Stress.**

Moving On

Frank found it difficult to believe that his last day had finally arrived. He had agonised over his decision to leave the Civil Service and all the friends he had made over a period of twenty years. Whilst it had taken him a couple of years to take the plunge, he had suddenly been filled with an overwhelming feeling of liberation, and an exhilarating sense of coming out of a long dark tunnel to encounter a new light...

As colleagues began to gather around Frank's desk to give him his farewell gifts and the traditional corny speech, Sue reflected on the forty years of moderately well paid tedium that she had endured. The oldest of old hands, she knew all the ropes which now pulled so tightly around her spirit. A new life beyond the world of work awaited her too of course, but the prospect of retirement left her gazing into the abyss, a blank canvass filling with horror and fear.

Louise frowned across at Frank and wondered why she was still here. She was younger than him and he had started a couple of years after her! She had left a message in his card, and donated a pound to the collection, but had never really liked the guy. He had always seemed a bit too aloof and self-satisfied to her. She had been the new girl once, and she now begrudged being regarded as an old hand. However, a smile started to flicker around her lips as she eyed up his chair and anticipated swiftly commandeering his impressive stock of stationery.

Story Telling Four

Mike was the first to grasp Frank's hand before his presentation. Tackling his first office job, the cold fear had quickly disappeared as he had warmed to the man who seemed to be quite content snuggling into his fifties with humour homespun and tinder-dry, a wry sceptic. Mike felt inspired by Frank's benevolence, his ongoing adoption of generations of Young Turks as he too now found himself approaching the stage of slightly world - weary, Wise Old Sage.

John checked his watch as he waited to start (he had a meeting in five minutes), trying to remember a few rehearsed pleasantries about this particular member of staff. He reflected that Frank seemed to be a man who was seldom praised, his voice never raised; probably unlikely to be missed, often dismissed as a safe pair of hands: rather bland, solid, not making a sound, always around, well-grounded .. Perhaps his departure might bring a few of then down to earth with a jerk - Who will listen to them, make the tea, finish off all their work?

... As colleagues dispersed, leaving him holding a large card and bottle of champagne, Frank looked at his almost-cleared desk, and suddenly felt a knot in his stomach, an empty flit-fluttering over toasting workmates and half-baked memories. The moment passed as his phone rang - He still had nearly half an hour to go before clocking-off. He dropped his glasses, rose-coloured, to the floor, then ground the glass underfoot.
Copyright Richard Seal 2017

I like this story perhaps it could be true but I think it is made up, in the original wording it was a lawyer perhaps it was just some rich person.

The Salvation Army realised that it had never received a donation from the city's most successful person. So a volunteer paid the individual a visit in his lavish office.

The volunteer opened the meeting by saying, 'Our research shows that even though your annual income is over two million dollars, you don't give a penny to charity. Wouldn't you like to give something back to your community?

The person thinks for a minute and says, 'First, did your research also show you that my mother is dying after a long painful illness, and she has huge medical bills that are far beyond her ability to pay?'

Embarrassed, the rep mumbles, 'Uh... No, I didn't know that.'

'Secondly,' says the rich person, 'did it show that my brother, a disabled Veteran, is blind and confined to a wheelchair and is unable to support his wife and six children?

The stricken rep begins to stammer an apology, but is cut off again...

'Thirdly, did your research also show you that my sister's husband died in a dreadful car accident, leaving her penniless with a mortgage and three children, one of whom is disabled and another that has learning disabilities requiring an array of private tutors?'

The humiliated rep, completely beaten, says, 'I'm so sorry. I had no idea.

And the rich person says, 'So, if I didn't give any money to them, what makes you think I'd give any to you?

- -

ATTORNEY: What gear were you in at the moment of the impact?
WITNESS: Gucci sweats and Reeboks.

ORDERING A PIZZA IN TODAY'S WORLD

Hello! Is this Gordon's Pizza?

    No sir, it's Google's Pizza

Did I dial the wrong number?

    No sir, Google bought the pizza store.

Oh, alright -then I'd like to place an order please.

    Do you want the usual?

The usual? You know what my usual is?

    According to the caller ID, the last 15 times you've ordered a 12-slice with double-cheese, sausage, and thick crust.

Okay - that's what I want this time too.

    May I suggest that this time you order an 8-slice with ricotta, arugula, and tomato instead?

No, I hate vegetables.

    But your cholesterol is not good.

How do you know?

    Through the subscribers guide We have the results of your blood tests for the last 7 years.

Maybe so, but I don't want the pizza you suggest – I already take medicine for high cholesterol.

But you haven't taken the medicine regularly. 4 months ago you purchased a box of only 30 tablets from Drugsale Network
I bought more from another drugstore.

It's not showing on your credit card sir.
 I paid in cash.

But according to your bank statement you did not withdraw that much cash.
 I have another source of cash

This is not showing on your last tax form, unless you got it from an undeclared income source.
 WHAT THE HELL? ENOUGH! I'm sick of Google, Facebook, Twitter, and WhatsApp. I'm going to an island without internet, where there's no cell phone line, and no one to spy on me

I understand sir, but you'll need to renew your passport ... it expired 5 weeks ago

---

ATTORNEY: Now doctor, isn't it true that when a person dies in his sleep, he doesn't know about it until the next morning? WITNESS: Did you actually pass the bar exam?

While looking at a house, my brother asked the
Real Estate agent which direction was north
because He didn't want the sun waking him up
every morning.
She asked, 'Does the sun rise in the north?'
My brother explained that the sun rises in the
east
And has for sometime. She shook her head and
said,
'Oh, I don't keep up with all that stuff......'
They Walk Among Us

A Father texts his son:
"My Dear Son,
Today is a day you will treasure for
all the days of your life. My best
love and good wishes, Your Father."
His Son texts back:
"Thanks Dad. But the wedding isn't
actually until tomorrow!"
His Father replies: "I know."

ATTORNEY: What was the first thing your
husband said to you that morning?
WITNESS: He said, 'Where am I, Cathy?'
ATTORNEY: And why did that upset you?
WITNESS: My name is Susan!

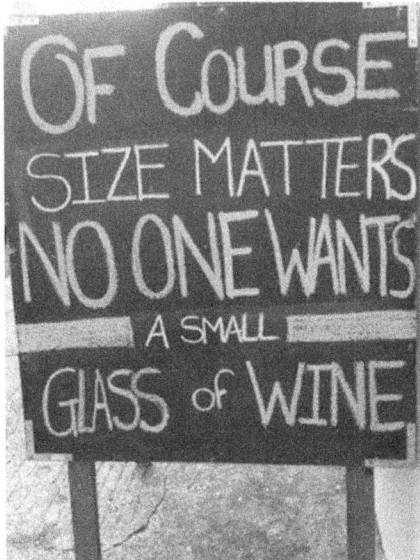

Hillary phoned the president's office shortly after midnight. "I need to talk to the president. It's an emergency!" exclaimed Hillary.
After some cajoling, the president's assistant agreed to wake him up. "So, what is it that's so important that it can't wait until morning?" grumbled Trump.

"A Supreme Court Judge just died, and I want to take his place," begged Hillary.

"Well, it's OK with me if it's OK with the mortuary," replied President Trump

This is a lovely true story written by ten year old Lily-Ella for a school project. We will be hearing more from her in coming issues of Story Telling. The original was in her hand writing, part of which is shown, it was typed out for clarity.

Lily-Ella Mainstone

Anne Frank

Annelies Frank is perhaps the most famous Jewish author across the World. She was born on 12th July 1929, Frankgurt, Germany. Her parents were called Otto and Edith Frank, she also had an older sister named Margot Frank. It was the time of peace before Hitler came to power in

Anne Franks

Annelis Frank is perhaps the most famous Jewish author across the world. She was born on the 12th July 1929, Frankfurt, Germany. Her parents were called Otto and Edith Frank, she also had an older sister named Margot Frank. It was the time of peace, before Hitler came to power in 1933. Before misery began.

Anne was an outgoing and curious child. She got into a lot of trouble at school far more than her quiet and serious older sister. Anne was more like her father whereas Margot was more like shy mother. When Anne was four her father decided they should move to Amsterdam, because of Hitler plotting to capture all the Jewish people in Germany.

Growing up, Anne had lots of friends. She liked to play hopscotch, hide and seek, tag and bike racing. Anne got into a lot of trouble at school, her teachers nicknamed her 'mistress chatterbox.' The Nazi's invaded Poland in 1939 and the Netherlands in 1940 and left the Jews in danger. In July 1942, Anne and her family moved to a new hideout, they called it 'the secret annex'. For her 13th Birthday Anne received a diary from her parents and decided to call it 'Kitty.' She named it Kitty after a friend it reminded her of. Each diary entry; she wrote, 'Dear Kitty. ' Anne wrote about all sorts of things, the first thing she wrote in it said, 'I hope you will be a great support and comfort to me.' The diary was green and red checked with gold edges.

Things continued to get worse, Hitler required that all Jews had to wear a yellow badge on their clothing. Some Jews were rounded to concentration camps. One day, a letter came through the post, it said Margot had to go to a labour camp. Otto was not going to let this happen. Otto and Edith decided to go to a new hideout, they told Anne and Margot to pack up their belongings and double up their clothing. Anne was upset as she wasn't allowed to bring her pet cat.

On the 6th July 1942, Anne and her family moved to a new hideout, 'the Secret annex,' but on the 5th July Margot had received a letter she had to report to the Nazi Political Police. Otto had been secretly preparing the Secret annex. Margot left first with Miep, the secretary, and then Anne and her parents left after them, so as there would be no suspicion. The annex had three small bedrooms, a tiny washroom and a large kitchen with a living room inside it. On the 13th July 1942 the Van Pels family joined the Frank family in the annex, they were also Jewish. The annex was behind a bookcase in a factory. Miep lived below and took food and clothes up to them.

On the morning of 24th June 1944, the Jews were captured. They were sent to Auschwitz Death Camp. A few weeks later the Franks and the Pels had to go to the Bergen-Belson Concentration camp, they travelled there by train. But the train was dark, cold and full of diseases. The camp was a horrible place and worse than the prison. Anne, Margot and Edith were split up with Otto. They didn't get any food and had to wear prison clothes, they had their hair cut really short, they had to walk bare foot everywhere on the hard ground and the Germans took away all their belongings. They slept in tiny tents on the floor.

Anne sadly died of Typhus, she will be remembered mostly by her diary.

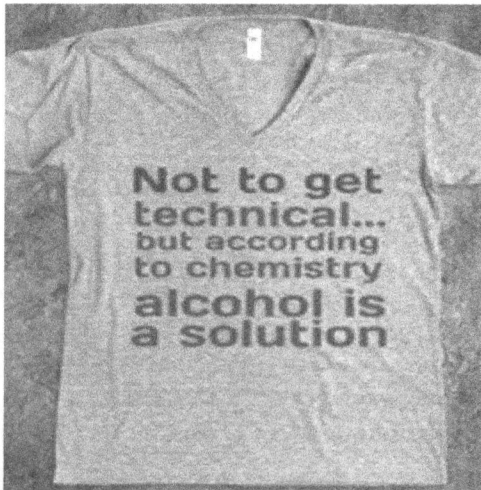

Then there is the story of the boy in the confessional! I should add the names are fictional

"Bless me Father, for I have sinned. I have been with a loose girl."

The priest asks, "Is that you, little Dominic Savino?"

"Yes, Father, it is."

"And who was the girl you were with?"

"I can't tell you, Father. I don't want to ruin her reputation."

"Well, Dominic, I'm sure to find out her name sooner or later so you may as well tell me now. Was it Tina Minetti?" "I cannot say."

"Was it Teresa Mazzarelli?" "I'll never tell."

"Was it Nina Capelli?" "I'm sorry, but I cannot name her."

"Was it Cathy Piriano?" "My lips are sealed."

"Was it Rosa DiAngelo, then?" "Please, Father, I cannot tell you."

The priest sighs in frustration. "You're very tight lipped, and I admire that. But you've sinned and have to atone. You cannot be an altar boy now for 4 months. Now you go and behave yourself."

Joey walks back to his pew, and his friend Franco slides over and whispers, "What'd you get?"

"Four months vacation and five good leads."

Quilt

Loved to embroider, stitched
together snatches of dreams,
fun fantasies, half-memories
gloss-enhanced, touched-up,
enlivened by passage of time,
into personal patchwork quilt,
with warmth and love, no guilt ..
Until one morning needle lost
in a haystack, no coming back
from that nightmare: long hair
sweat-matted, tears streaming,
waking up in terror, screaming.

Copy right Richard Seal 2016

You shed more than 1 million skin cells every single day but they are constantly replenished automatically, to save you from turning transparent and becoming rather exposed! Your skin is actually an organ; in fact it's the largest organ you have, with a surface area of 18 square feet (2 square meters).

I was always taught to respect my elders.
But it keeps getting harder to find one.

Dear alcohol,

We had a deal that you would make me prettier, funnier and a better dancer.

I saw the video, we need to talk.

Rebuilding New Orleans after Katrina often caused residents to be challenged to prove home titles going back hundreds of years. That is because of community history stretching back over two centuries during which houses were passed along through generations of family, sometimes making it quite difficult to establish a paper trail of ownership.

Later in Life

HAVE YOU EVER BEEN GUILTY OF LOOKING AT OTHERS YOUR OWN AGE AND THINKING, SURELY I CAN'T LOOK THAT OLD?

MY NAME IS ALICE SMITH AND I WAS SITTING IN THE WAITING ROOM FOR MY FIRST APPOINTMENT WITH A NEW DENTIST.

I NOTICED HIS DDS DIPLOMA, WHICH BORE HIS FULL NAME.

SUDDENLY, I REMEMBERED A TALL, HANDSOME, DARK-HAIRED BOY WITH THE SAME NAME HAD BEEN IN MY HIGH SCHOOL CLASS SOME 50+ YEARS AGO.

COULD HE BE THE SAME GUY THAT I HAD A SECRET CRUSH ON, WAY BACK THEN?

UPON SEEING HIM, HOWEVER, I QUICKLY DISCARDED ANY SUCH THOUGHT.

THIS BALDING, GRAY-HAIRED MAN WITH THE DEEPLY LINED FACE WAS WAY TOO OLD TO HAVE BEEN MY CLASSMATE.

AFTER HE EXAMINED MY TEETH, I ASKED HIM IF HE HAD ATTENDED MORGAN PARK HIGH SCHOOL.

"YES. YES, I DID. I'M A MUSTANG," HE GLEAMED WITH PRIDE.

"WHEN DID YOU GRADUATE?" I ASKED.

HE ANSWERED, "IN 1962. WHY DO YOU ASK?"

"YOU WERE IN MY CLASS!" I EXCLAIMED.

HE LOOKED AT ME CLOSELY.

THEN, THAT UGLY, OLD, BALD, WRINKLED, FAT ASS, GRAY-HAIRED, DECREPIT SON-OF-A-BITCH ASKED ME,

.. "WHAT DID YOU TEACH?" .

**The following is the opening chapter of 'Felix Wild'
(ISBN 978-1-911105-21-3) a historic novel written by
Peter Broadbent to be published in Hardback in June
2017 by Chaplin Books**
(http://www.chaplinbooks.co.uk) 5 Carlton Way,
Gosport, Hampshire PO12 1LN Tel +44(0)23 9252
9020. Contact Amanda Field.
© Peter Broadbent

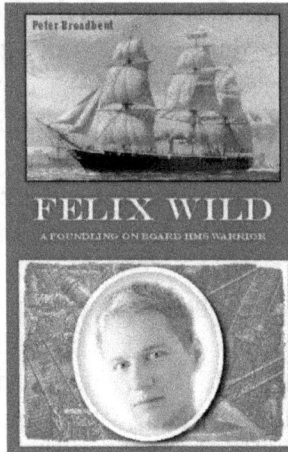

Chapter 1
PETTY SESSIONS

The lock on the courthouse door is bothersome stiff.
Cobbled together many years ago by an incompetent
local blacksmith, it is particularly stubborn at this time of
year.

Ben Nettlebed, a skeletal man unable to apply muscle
of any kind, has to use a well-practised combination of
knee, scrawny elbow and malnourished shoulder to grind
the lock open. Ben has clawed a living in and around the
town all his life. He has no family or friends and knows

nothing of his parents. Today he will earn seven-pence and a farthing.

The north-west wind brings with it a driving rain. The Monday mob, who are keen to witness the castigation of local scoundrels, jostle each other to squeeze through the narrow doorway from Bemisters Lane. They respectfully allow a tall gentleman, wearing a well-tailored coat and silk top-hat, to be the first through the door.

Inside the courthouse the tall gentleman flicks moisture from the shoulders of his cape, lays his fox-head cane on one of the three cushioned chairs in the centre of the front row of public seats, and sits himself down. Behind him, the clamour for the best places on the bare-wood benches is becoming increasingly raucous and ill-mannered.

The courthouse has been closed for a month and the atmosphere is stale and damp. The walls are hung with sagging drapes that hide the cracked and peeling plaster. Ben tugs on a hemp rope and, with an audible whimper, a small window high in the north wall opens slightly. He secures the end of the rope around a protruding rusted nail and turns to watch the familiar Gosport faces scramble for the few spots still available against the wall nearest to the front.

Without a cloth to swab his running nose, Ben turns to face the wall and hurriedly wipes his nose on the sleeve of his threadbare coat. He isn't looking forward to serving the Justice-of-the-Day today: he knows from experience that Justice Lionel Braveheart enjoys a tipple or two, and hurries through his Sessional duties so that he can finish before midday.

Attached to the courthouse is a partially roofed, red-bricked courtyard with high walls and a stout wooden entrance door secured by a robust black-iron bar. Around all four walls runs a bare wooden bench, occupied by those unfortunates who have been dragged or summoned to attend today's Petty Sessions. Hunched on the bench are twenty or so cold, wet and shabbily dressed individuals, most staring at the rain puddling on the red tiled floor. Some are fettered by hands or feet. The increasingly heavy rain is drenching those who are sitting on the benches where the overhead cover is in need of repair. In each corner, under a triangular roof section of sorts, stands a Constable of the law clutching a wooden truncheon.

A young boy, sitting next to an elderly man cradling a thin roll of papers, is scanning the walls to see if there is a possible means of escape.

An old woman tries to stuff the end of a cracked clay pipe in her mouth but her gnarled hands make it difficult. The hacking cough of a man with rags on his feet goes on too long and he is lifted up by one of the Constables who slaps him hard on his back. His coughing stops and he falls to his knees.

'Toby, you old coiler, the last time you was 'ere we thought we'd seen the last of you,' says the Constable, tossing him back to his seat on the bench. 'Better ask the Justice to have you up early. In case you don't last the full day.'

Toby inhales deeply; his breath rattles audibly.

'You ferk ... You ferk ...'

The Constable points his truncheon menacingly at Toby's gulping throat.

'Careful what you says to me, Toby old man. I could 'ave a mind to convey your 'ostility to Justice Braveheart.'

'Justice Braveheart is a drunk with bollicks for brains.' Toby taps his chest. 'I knows all about Justice Brave ...'

The truncheon raps across one of Toby's elderly knees, bringing tears to his eyes. He gives a pained yelp.

An elderly woman swathed in numerous layers of red checked material and wearing a soiled bonnet is scratching her swollen ankle: one of the rope-like veins oozes blood.

Inside the courthouse, Ben places the Justice's desk and the lecterns for the two Clerks in their customary position. From a box he spreads sweet-smelling herbs around the Justice's desk: a requirement of Justice Braveheart who complains bitterly of the stench and possible contagion of the room.

The Junior Clerk, wearing the black cloak and headgear peculiar to those who are legally trained, appears and places three leather-bound books on the Justice's desk. He puts a polished round stone of brown agate alongside.

'We have old Toby again,' Ben says to the Clerk. 'He's coughing up bad in the yard.'

The Clerk nods and busies himself with his folder of papers. Ben sniffs: he understands that Clerks of the Sessions, even the junior ones, don't pay him any mind. He wipes his nose on his sleeve again. At his grey-stubbled age he would appreciate some level of respect, despite his rather humble position. How he dislikes this seven-penny job and everyone associated with it.

A small steaming rivulet of bright yellow piss snakes across the red-brick courtyard floor. It puddles a few feet away from the feet of the adjacent policeman. An elderly be whiskered woman, with a square of grey material on her balding head, bunches up her skirt with her gnarled hands and smiles in relief. Sitting next to her, a bearded man with ragged holes in both of his trouser knees places a grubby hand in her lap.

The door from the courthouse creaks opens and the Junior Clerk scans those assembled. There is a stiffening of the Constables.

'The Justice is not here yet,' says the Clerk, looking at nobody in particular.

'Whose papers are on top of the pile, Clerk?' asks a Constable.

'The boy maybe, because of his years.'

The young boy understands that he has little time to make his escape.

Justice Braveheart, dressed in a fashionable, but badly creased full-length tailcoat, a beaver top-hat and hessian boots, arrives at a shuffle. He is followed by his Senior Clerk carrying a folder of papers secured with a variety of coloured ribbons.

The Justice passes Ben without acknowledging him. Ben watches as the Senior Clerk places the ribboned papers on the desk. The Justice slides the books to the side of his desk and places a fist-sized stone, carved in the shape of a skull, on the top of his papers. He sniffs and wipes his nose with a clean handkerchief as he scans the topmost paper.

'An unknown boy of unknown years, of unknown parentage and ... oh shit.'

'A young Gosport boy sir, not yet a shaver.' The Junior Clerk, standing erect behind his lectern explains, respectfully bowing his head.

Justice Braveheart fingers through the top few sheets and extracts the one he is looking for.

'While I am on my feet I will deal with the latest misdemeanour enacted by that out-and-out rascal James Wheelwright. Fetch the guilty bastard in now!'

The erect, unwashed, unshaven and bare-footed James Wheelwright is escorted into the room by a pair of Constables. All three take up position facing Justice Braveheart. The mumble of expectancy from the crowded public benches gradually settles to a hum. Those who are unseated lean up against the walls: the stench of wet, unwashed clothing is overwhelming.

'Accused, state your name and age for the record,' says the Junior Clerk.

'Mister James Wheelwright aged thirty-one years,' says the accused in a low, gravelly voice.

'Abode?'

'No abode, if you mean a place to live. I don't have a place to ferkin live.'

'Language!' shouts the Senior Clerk.

'Language, Wheelwright!' bellows Justice Braveheart. 'If you choose to use intemperate language in my courtroom, I shall send you overseas where you can blaspheme away to your heart's content to those of a similar nature.'

A Constable jabs the accused in the ribs with his truncheon.

'Say "sorry sir".'

'Sorry sir,' mumbles James Wheelwright.

Justice Braveheart looks up. 'The title "Mister" does not sit well with you, Wheelwright: I shall have it removed from the record.' He flicks open a paper and reads. 'James Wheelwright, labourer of Gosport, you are charged by Diantha Cooke single woman of Gosport, to have had carnal knowledge of her personal body without her consent and to have gotten her with child. This child when born will be a bastard and thereby chargeable to the town.' The Justice places his paper to the right of his desk. 'James Wheelwright, you shall formally appear at the forthcoming Quarter Sessions to answer this charge. Until such time you will be detained locally and work daily with the Haslar gravediggers. May the winter's ground frost be hard, deep and back-breaking. Take the cock-happy bastard away.' He hands the charge sheet to the Junior Clerk as James Wheelwright is dragged away.

'Is the woman Diantha Cooke present?' the Justice asks the room.

Silence.

'Never in attendance when we need to talk to the strumpet,' he mumbles as he accepts a folded sheet of paper from the Senior Clerk.

The young boy is brought in, flanked by two Constables: all three stand a few paces inside the door. The Senior Clerk opens a box, untangles and finger-combs a lengthy article of straw-coloured headgear and hands it deferentially to Justice Braveheart who places it on his head. He adjusts the headgear, adopts a self-important stance, unfolds the paper and reads in well-modulated tones. 'I, as the duly appointed Justice of the

Peace for Gosport in the County of Hampshire, do hereby declare the Petty Session for Monday the nineteenth day of November in the year of our Lord eighteen hundred and sixty, open. I trust that I will not experience a repeat of the distractions caused during my previous visit.' He turns his sheet of paper over. 'I remind you of the commemoration of the Feast of the visitation of Mary with Elizabeth as recorded in the Gospel of Luke. Elizabeth is with child courtesy of John the Baptist.' He ruffles the sheet of paper and tosses it onto his desk. 'This commemoration is completely outdated, Clerk. I am minded that I read the exact same words months past ... you incompetent.'

The Senior Clerk shuffles away to a shadowed corner and removes his headgear.

The young boy leans towards the door, making ready to run. He is restrained by the larger of the two Constables.

Justice Braveheart looks at the boy, coughs and waves his papers.

'We have a busy day ahead of us, let us continue.' He glares at those on the public benches. 'Everybody stand ... stand!'

While waiting for everybody to get to their feet he fingers his papers and plays with his stone skull. He coughs loudly. 'Long live Queen Victoria and her husband ... bless him for his support and fortitude. All be seated, and refrain from your blasted coughing if you are able!'

There is a rustle from the assembled throng as they seat themselves. Someone coughs. Justice Braveheart wipes his brow with his handkerchief and plucks a stray frond from his headgear.

'I expect all persons in this place to uphold the law of assembly as defined by myself. I shall not hesitate to punish anybody who disobeys any of my rulings.'

The young boy flanked by the two Constables shuffles his bare feet.

'I have a mind to deal with all today's matters in a swift and unbending manner. I expect quick and accurate recording from the Clerks and the collection of any monies as required. Place the first good-for-nothing troublemaker in front of me so that I can see his eyes.'

The small boy is pushed to a position directly facing the Justice's desk and is told to stand up straight.

The Justice looks glaringly at the boy. 'Name?'

The boy looks at the floor.

'No name sir,' replies the Junior Clerk. 'The boy has no recorded name.' 'We need a name, man,' says the Justice, fixing the Junior Clerk with a steely eye. 'Can't discipline anyone without a blasted name.'

'The accused is an unnamed vagrant, sir. We believe that he is without parents, siblings or close friends. The charge papers show that he was given the name Felix by the authorities as he was arrested for a minor misdemeanour earlier this year on Saint Felix Day, the eighth day of March sir.' *Peter Braodbents story will be continued in the next issue 'Story Telling Five'.*

The song Auld Lang Syne is sung at the stroke of midnight in almost every English-speaking country in the world to bring in the new year.

THIS COULD BE US SOMEDAY!

A couple in their nineties are both having problems remembering things. During a check-up, the doctor told them that they're physically okay, but they might want to start writing things down to help them remember.

Later that night, while watching TV, the old man got up from his chair. 'Want anything while I'm in the kitchen?' he asks.

'Will you get me a bowl of ice cream?'

'Sure.'

'Don't you think you should write it down so you can remember it?' she asks.

'No, I can remember it.'

'Well, I'd like some strawberries on top, too. Maybe you should write it down, so as not to forget it?'

He says, 'I can remember that. You want a bowl of ice cream with strawberries.'

'I'd also like whipped cream. I'm certain you'll forget that, write it down?' she asks.

Irritated, he says, 'I don't need to write it down, I can remember it! Ice cream with strawberries and whipped cream - I got it, for goodness sake!'

Then he toddles into the kitchen. After about 20 minutes, the old man returns from the kitchen and hands his wife a plate of bacon and eggs. She stares at the plate for a moment.

'Where's my toast?'

~ ~

A man spoke frantically into the phone: 'My wife is pregnant and her contractions are only two minutes apart'. 'Is this her first child?' the doctor asked. *'No!' the man shouted, 'This is her husband!'*

This was sent to Story Telling by a friend and as you will see below there is a disproportion of people with NO CHILDREN! Read on.

Hmmmmm........interesting?

One noteworthy reality about Europe's current political leadership is summarised here by Phil Lawler:

• Macron, the newly elected French president, has no children.
• German chancellor Angela Merkel has no children.
• British prime minister Theresa May has no children.
• Italian prime minister Paolo Gentiloni has no children.
• Holland's Mark Rutte,
• Sweden's Stefan Löfven,
• Luxembourg's Xavier Bettel,
• Scotland's Nicola Sturgeon—all have no children.
• Jean-Claude Juncker, president of the European Commission, has no children.

"So a grossly disproportionate number of the people making decisions about Europe's future have no direct personal stake in that future."

The British have such a command of decorum and aplomb to which we can only aspire.

This message is from Ray Enos and for his friends who appreciate the finer points of the English language used correctly:

His Lordship was in the study when the butler approached and coughed discreetly.
May I ask you a question, My Lord?"

"Go ahead, Carson ," said His Lordship.
"I am doing the crossword in The Times and found a word the exact meaning of which I am not too certain."

"What word is that?" asked His Lordship.
"APLOMB," My Lord.

"Now that's a difficult one to explain. I would say it is self-assurance or complete composure."
"Thank you, My Lord, but I'm still a little confused about it."

"Let me give you an example to make it clearer. Do you remember a few months ago when the Duke and Duchess of Cambridge arrived to spend a weekend with us?"
"I remember the occasion very well, My Lord. It gave the staff and myself much pleasure to look after them."

"Also," continued the Earl of Grantham, "do you remember when Will plucked a rose for Kate in the rose garden?"

"I was present on that occasion, My Lord, ministering to their needs.

"While Will was plucking the rose, a thorn embedded itself in his thumb very deeply."

"I witnessed the incident, My Lord, and saw the Duchess herself remove the thorn and bandage his thumb with her own dainty handkerchief."

"That evening the hole the rose made in his thumb was very sore. Kate had to cut his venison for him even though it was extremely tender."

"Yes, My Lord, I did see everything that transpired that evening."

"And do you remember the next morning while you were pouring coffee for Her Ladyship, Kate inquired of Will in a loud voice, "Darling, does your prick still throb?" and you, Carson, did not spill one drop of coffee?

That, Carson is **aplomb**."

~ ~

Two guys were discussing popular family trends on sex, marriage, and family values..

Bill said, 'I didn't sleep with my wife before we got married, did you?'

Larry replied, 'I'm not sure, what was her maiden name?'

A Homeless Guy..

A homeless guy is traveling down a country lane, tired and hungry he comes across a Pub called the "George and the Dragon."

Although it's late and the Pub is closed he knocks on the door. The innkeeper's wife sticks her head out of a window.

"Could I have some food?" he asks. The woman glances at his shabby clothes and obviously poor condition and sternly says, "No!"

"Any chance of a pint of ale then?"

"No!" she says again.

"Could I at least sleep in your barn?"

"No!" By this time, she was shouting. The down-and-out says, "OK Then Might I please...?"

"What now?" the woman shouts impatiently.

"Might I please have a word with George?

Warm Wisdom

It had been such a long time since the brothers had last met, and yet when he embarked on the thankless task of clearing the old family home, Nick found so many reminders of his younger sibling. When looking through one of the cupboards in the hall he flashed a smile at finding an old hot water bottle. The brothers had waged frequent bed battles to decide who would be the one lucky enough to capture its scalding warmth, while the next morning had invariably brought cold toes or wet sheets with the stopper rolling loose. He held Jim close for a moment, somehow still here in this fractured rubber, coated in dust.

Finding the old cheese grater, Nick was back in the kitchen with mum. As a young child he had offered to help her to wash up, but felt mortified, while stood by her side, when breaking her favourite gravy boat. He was so distraught, but thanks to his brother, he soon became smug - naughty Jim had burned her best rug!

Seeing one of Jim's old guitars reminded Nick of the special 'gift' that both of them had inherited from her: singing voices which could strip paint, their warbling jarring setting teeth on edge. Only by lip synching at weddings and funerals could they avoid the a scritch-scratch screech: siblings truly united in discordant dissonance.

Stepping outside into the overgrown garden took Nick back to that childhood occasion when they had excitedly cleared a large patch of weeds, getting stung by nettles in the process. As they plunged the spade into soft soil the adrenalin surged.

The brothers had put their hopes and dreams, wide-eyed and earnest, into a time capsule. Five years on they found the box's lid cracked and mush slush swirling ... It did not dampen deepening bonds, while hysterical laughter lifted the sad moment. Catapulting a bucket of mud, wet leaves and twigs onto their sister's head had had a similar effect, although smiles had frozen on seeing her running to tell mum ...

At the brothers' long-awaited reunion next day, Nick's laughter lines are met by Jim's crow's feet, his big eyes still wide and blue, and their tight embrace evokes the old photograph which resided on the sideboard - they are the little boys stranding on the beach in red shirts and blue shorts, arms around each other's shoulders. Lingering, reluctant to break the hug, Nick wonders how their adult conversation might compare to those discussions between pillow fighting bouts, midnight musings after bouncing on their beds ... Perhaps their seeds of warm wisdom and jubilant joy of life were sown when Santa sat beside the Tooth Fairy.

Copyright Richard Seal 2017

~ ~

We're four jolly sailors, some sailors are we,
 We love to sail upon the sea,
And watch the sunrise as it blazes
Through our alcoholic hazes

THIS TIME PERIOD.

THE YEAR IS 1917
This will boggle your mind!
"One hundred years ago". What a difference a century makes! Here are some statistics for that Year.

The average life expectancy for men was 47 years.
Fuel for cars was sold in chemists only.
Only 14 percent of the homes had a bath.
Only 8 percent of the homes had a telephone.
The maximum speed limit in most cities was 10 mph.
The tallest structure in the world was the Eiffel Tower.
The average British wage in 1915 was £15 per year!
A competent accountant could expect to earn £800 per year. A dentist £900 per year. A vet between £600 and £900 per year. And a mechanical engineer about £2000 per year.
More than 95 percent of all births took place at home.
Ninety percent of all Doctors had no university education! Instead, they attended so-called medical schools, many of which were condemned in the press AND the government as "substandard."
Sugar cost two pence a pound.
Eggs were 10 pence a dozen.
Coffee was five pence a pound.
Most women only washed their hair once a month, and used Borax or egg yolks for shampoo.
Canada passed a law that prohibited poor people from entering into their country for any reason.

The five leading causes of death were:
1. Pneumonia and influenza...2. Tuberculosis...
3. Diarrhoea...4. Heart disease...5. Stroke
The American flag had 45 stars.
The population of Las Vegas, Nevada was only 30.
Crossword puzzles, canned beer, and iced tea hadn't been invented yet.
There was neither a Mother's Day nor a Father's Day.
Two out of every 10 adults couldn't read or write and only 6 per cent of all British pupils went to university.
Marijuana, heroin, and morphine were all available over the counter at local corner chemists. Back then chemists said, "Heroin clears the complexion, gives buoyancy to the mind, regulates the stomach, bowels, and is, in fact, a perfect guardian of health!"
The licensing act was brought in to restrict Public Houses opening times so as to protect workers, who were manufacturing shells for the Great War, from drinking in excess minimising the risk of explosions in the munitions work due to the workforce having imbibed too much alcohol.
Eighteen percent of households had at least one full-time servant or domestic help...
There were about 230 reported murders in the ENTIRE U.S.A.! In 2014 this figure has risen to 14,249.
In the UK the murder rate in 1915 was 1420. In 2015 it was 537. (Perhaps we are doing something right!)

- -

Relationships are a lot like algebra. Have you ever looked at your X and wondered Y?

Percy's latest novel 'The Cormack's is now available through Amazon and other outlets. It is a thrilling story with a very surprising end. Percy says no one will guess it even when they are down to the last twenty pages.

The lead in to the story follows.

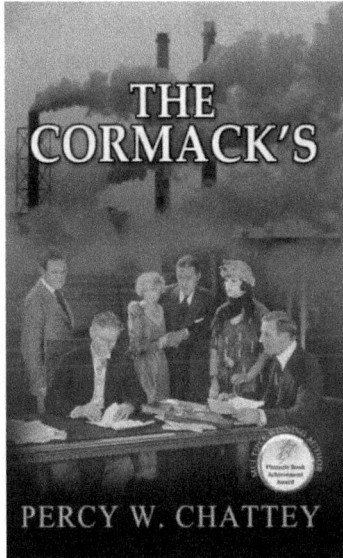

Bertram Miles

Bristol, England February 1920

The church bells across the City of Bristol were vying with each other in declaring it was six o'clock in the evening on this cold wet nightfall in February. St John the Baptist Church, part of the nine hundred year old Municipality Gates, was the last to broadcast.

Nearby in one of the old cobbled streets as the echo of the bells died away, a single occupant sat at a desk in the small bureau, set in a row of similar terraced offices. On its windows in gold leaf the words declaring Bert Miles Estate Agents. The middle aged man of medium build, sporting a full beard, was busy calculating how much money he had accumulated in his short stay in the city.

It had all been very easy, too easy some would say as he had perpetrated a similar dishonest scam. It was one he had used around the country and not caring who he hurt in his activities. He would stay for short periods in one place advertising cheap nonexistent properties, taking deposits and then moving on before being found out.

He looked up at the wall clock with its loud tick keeping pace with time and was surprised at its reading wondering if he had wound the spring up that morning as it seemed to be a little slow. Taking a glistening gold fob watch, on a chain from his waistcoat pocket he checked it to see if they agreed. Looking through dimpled glazing of the office windows into the street he was disappointed to see the skies had clouded over and it was starting to rain which would mean a wet ride back to the small Inn he was staying at, some few miles away on the Bath Road.

He could not see the point in staying waiting for a customer, which on a wet afternoon was not very likely, when instead he could be in the warmth of the hotel lounge with his favourite brew in one hand, and the other being warmed by the fire.

With this thought in mind he went to the rear of the property to the stable where that morning he had secured his horse in the comfort of the sheltered area. The tall black stallion turned its head away from the feed and looked at him in a knowing way, as he retrieved the saddle from the wall mounting and placed it on the animals back.

A short time later he was back in the small room to the rear of his office preparing himself for the evening ride. The small automatic pistol hanging in its holster on the wall, he would strap on before leaving for the feeling of security it offered when travelling.

He heard the tinkle of the bell attached to the outside door as it opened from the street. He was a little disappointed as he was looking forward to leaving and returning to the comfort of his lodgings. Going through the low narrow door, leading to the small bureau in the front, he sensed trouble when he saw two men looking very serious. Beyond, and outside the property, a policeman standing upright and straight, with his back to the glass panelling to the front of the property, close to the door to the street.

At first they did not say anything; they were looking around the room as if it was more important than what they had to say. The smaller of the two looked at him and spoke in an educated voice, the words were pronounced flawlessly and clearly.

Instantly he recognised him as a man he had taken a substantial sum of money off for a property which existed, but he had no authority to sell it. At the time he had seen it as a wonderful opportunity when the prospective client came into the office waving an advert, by another Estate agent of a property he wanted to buy.

Miles had seen it as a possibility of making some easy money and had falsely said he had been instructed to sell the house. After he had assured the person that it was a very popular district and that many people were looking and interested in it, as a result he had taken a substantial deposit off the man.

"My name is Mr Perkins, you must remember me as recently I came to you following a property which was advertised in Clifton, which I agreed to buy. I and my wife deposited with you a substantial sum of money as a deposit. But there seems to be a serious mistake as the people living there say 'yes they want to sell, but they have no agreement to sell it with you'."

He remembered it well as it had only been the week previously. Perkins, he had found at the time was a little gullible even though he owned the large hardware shop in the City Centre. Although it had been a risk as the sale was bogus, he had rejoiced at the time thinking it would be the icing on the cake of the scams he had concluded whilst in the city, as he knew it was getting to the time to move on and set up again in another populace.

This was the last thing Miles had expected, these people calling on him. He smiled "Yes, I remember very well, and as you say there has been a mistake and I was going to call on you this evening to sort the matter out with you." His voice had mimicked the others.

The other well dressed person spoke still wearing his bowler hat, which Bertram had thought unusual as it would have been normal for him to have removed it "My name is Sergeant Hales from Bridemead Police Station, as you say you were prepared to visit Mr Perkins this evening then Sir, I require you to accompany me to the Station, when there you can explain your actions."

Bertram was in shock he realised he had not been as careful as he normally was. He should have got the agreement from the sellers first, before taking the Perkins money that way he would be long gone before the owners of the house started asking for their funds as he would not have passed the deposit on. "Your money is in the other office." He indicated by nodding his head towards the room behind him. "If you would follow me then we can retrieve it." He had another thought, and feeling stupid about his decision, out of bravado, to use his own name. Why he had he could not remember as in the past he had always used an alias. Now, when he escaped from this interview they would know who to look for.

He turned trying to show the confidence he did not feel, looking over his shoulder he saw they were following with the policeman leading the way. On entering the room he quickly slid the small gun out of its holster. Palming it in his hand he said "It is through here." Pointing to the rear door which lead out to the stables. As he stepped through it the policeman realised he was trying to escape and shouted "Stop right there, and turn around."

A smile crept across Miles face and he turned sharply raising his hand and pointing the small pistol at the group coming through the doorway. The Policeman's face changed into a shocked look, he stopped and then held out his arms pushing the others back.

Miles continued pointing the pistol at his followers and pulled the trigger. It was with satisfaction when he saw the bullets hit the law man in the chest. Before the others had a chance to react he dragged his outer coat off a hook, picking up his briefcase and quickly made his way to the rear. Slamming the door he went through the small scullery. He removed the key from the mortise lock of the outer door and was through it into the rear a moment later. He turned and with the key he locked the door from the outside.

- -

Did you know that Dolphins are so smart that within a few weeks of captivity,_they can train people to stand on the very edge of the pool and throw them fish?

~~~~~~

Not Heard

The boy looked up at his mother, trying hard to catch her attention, tears beginning to prickle in his rubbed eyes .. It was to prove unwise to try interrupting her while she was occupied with her mobile phone, sending a message to a friend attaching pictures of her new shoes .. Seeing red, she swatted at the pesky child muttering hotly to herself 'Oh why can children these days never keep themselves amused?'

The little lad stood shocked at seeing his mother turn into a monster, her eyes replaced by flames, with a flushed red face. His sister stared down at her ice cream cone while he suffered alone, feeling a sharp smack which caused him to spill half his coke down his teeshirt. It was no joke - What was it all for? All he did was try to ask her nicely if he could have a straw ...

Rueful after her son had sent her past the point of no return once again - sadly a familiar refrain - Jane recalled vowing as a child not to repeat her parents' tired phrases, yet when reaching a flashpoint the language always fails and good intentions are derailed - she turns into her mother in the mad moment ... Then again, she reflects, is it really so absurd for kids to be seen but not heard?

Copyright Richard Seal 2017

The First Text Message

Dear John, this is Alan next door. I am sorry buddy, but I have a confession to make to you. I've been riddled with guilt these past few months and have been trying to pluck up the courage to tell you to your face, but I am at least now telling you in text as I can't live with myself a moment longer without you knowing.

The truth is, I have been sharing your wife, day and night when you're not around. In fact, probably more than you. I haven't been getting it at home recently, but that's no excuse I know. The temptation was just too much. I can no longer live with the guilt and I hope you will accept my sincerest apologies and forgive me.

I promise that it won't happen again.

Please come up with a fee for usage, and I'll pay you.

Regards, Alan.

The Response

John, feeling insulted and betrayed, grabbed his gun, stomped next door and shot his neighbour dead. He returned home, poured himself a stiff drink and went out into the garden for some fresh air. He took out his phone where he saw he had a subsequent message from his neighbour.

The Second Text Message

Hi John, This is Alan next door again. Sorry about the slight typo on my last text. I expect you worked it out anyway, but as I'm sure you noticed that my smart phone's Autocorrect feature changed "Wi-Fi" to "Wife". Technology hey?? Hope you saw the funny side of that.

Regards, Alan.

The Power Cut

We had a power cut at our house this morning and my PC, laptop, TV, DVD, iPad & my new surround sound music system were all shut down.
Then I discovered that my mobile phone battery was dead and to top it off it was raining outside, so I couldn't play golf.
I went into the kitchen to make coffee and then I remembered that this also needs power, so I sat and talked with my wife for a couple of hours.

She seems like a nice person...!!

- -

Subject: Beer

There's a big brewers convention going on in Sydney and head brewers are congregated from all over the world.

Come break time they pop out to the bar for a wet.
The bloke from Budweiser orders a Bud.
The bloke from Carleton orders a Hahn Super Dry
The bloke from Castlemain orders a XXXX
The bloke from Heineken orders a Heineken
The bloke from Steinlager orders a Steinlager
The bloke from Carlsberg orders a Carlsberg
and the bloke from Guinness orders a lemonade.

They all look at him shocked and one of the blokes asks, "Hey, how come you're not drinking beer?"

Paddy turns and looks at him and replies, "Well as none of you lot are I thought it best to abstain too"

Melon Man

**Walking, keeping eye
out for kids, one running
ahead, other lagging
behind, see man lost
in a watermelon slice.
Luxuriating in moment
of red juice dripping, pip
dropping lusciousness,
living like last moments,
loving his final meal.**
Copyright Richard Seal 2017

~~~~~~

The Chauffer

I had spent the morning cleaning the 1936 jet black Rolls Royce I drive, a beautiful car with a cocktail cabinet in the rear which was ideal for weddings, and that was the journey today. The wedding was at Caxton Hall in the centre of London. First I was due to pick up the wedding party in Essex, after which take the bride and groom from the famous wedding facility near Westminster, and take them out to Hertfordshire for the wedding reception.

It was a very hot day when we arrived at this large house where the party was to be held, and as I had to wait to take some people back to Essex, I was invited in.

On a reception table taking up one side of the room, was the Wedding Cake and the buffet,. There was also about a dozen bottles of Champagne, which someone had removed the wires from the corks, before the guests had arrived. I guess so it could be poured out quickly on their arrival. As I said it was a warm day with the sun shining through the window and on to the table, and although it looked grand with the bottles glistening in the light. Then again the pressure in the bottles was rising….

On arrival the form was for the guest to go into the reception area so as to greet the bride and her new husband. I was standing to one side when the happy couple came into where the people were gathered. The bride, still in her white flowing wedding outfit came into the room arm in arm with her new husband all smiles and laughter. The couple moved over to the table to admire the cake and layout and were standing next to it.

There was a loud 'POP', and then another as one by one all the bottles blew their corks out with champers jetting into the air hitting the ceiling and flooding the table and going all over the place; I was still laughing when I got home. I think somebody learned a lesson that day as to why champagne bottles have wires on them.
Copyright www.percychatteybooks.com

- -

ATTORNEY: What is your date of birth?
WITNESS: July 18th.
ATTORNEY: What year?
WITNESS: Every year.

A very good question!

A young Arab asks his father, "What is that weird hat you are wearing?"

The father said, "Why, it's a 'chechia' because in the desert it protects our heads from the sun."

"And what is this type of clothing that you are wearing?" asked the young man.

"It's a 'djbellah' because in the desert it is very hot and it protects the body." said the father.

The son asked, "And what about those ugly shoes on your feet?

His father replied, "These are 'babouches', which keep us from burning
our feet in the desert."

"So tell me then," added the boy.

"Yes, my son?"

"Why are you living in London and still wearing all this stuff?"

~~~~~~

T he Importance of Walking

Walking can add minutes to your life.
This enables you at 85 years old to spend an additional 5 months in a nursing home at $7000 per month..

Sorry my Child we did you wrong.

Yes my child we got it wrong, we leave you a world not of love, but hate.

Every day we looked on you with affection and wonderment.

We did not understand as time went past it was becoming too late

Our indulgence was of leisure, cartoon characters, football and fun.

With open arms we accepted the newbie's into our lives as one.

The future was bright and in no need of our care.

Sorry child we did you wrong.

The churches in our communities standing upright and tall.

The visit on the Sunday dressed in our best as we prayed to be loved by all.

But the all became the box in the corner with pictures to lure us away

And a new prayer to sit in comfort and be shown a different way.

While we allowed to be swayed by programmes not of our choosing.

We did not notice the newbie's changed our precious churches to our losing.

The future was bright and in no need of our care.

Sorry child we did you wrong.

Through that indulgence we showered you with love and affection.

With all Sunday teachings long forgotten replaced by gluttony and greed as a selection.

We taught air travel, flash cars and burglar alarms but not how to secure the country's borders.
 We allowed communities to disappear the butcher, the baker and the milkman in the morn who used to take our orders.
The High Street now empty, replaced by a conglomerate with trolleys to fill,
Readily to take your money quickly at their till.
The future was bright and in no need of our care.
Sorry child we did you wrong.

To understand our negligence we had fresh memories of our loved ones
and their sufferings in a terrible war that burned the ground,
Death and destruction at every turn; hardship by the tonnes
lack of supplies, food, water and certainly not a sweet to be found.
The new spring that blossomed in the decades following this horror,
 led to an extravagance never seen before
And a need to ensure our children would never have to borrow
Or repeat these things that would shake them to the core.
The future was bright and in no need of our care.
Sorry child we did you wrong

Now new horrors are striking the world, different from the World at War although the same.
Another enemy but within; the newbie's we welcomed with open arms who have taught us to play their game.
Governments allowing schools to air brush History into something which was not.

Churchill, Trafalgar and Waterloo confined to the dustbin whilst trying to find a new way; which is now what we have got.

Sorry my Child we let you down,
Now it is your turn, perhaps you will want to turn it around.

Copyright Percy W. Chattey 2017

~ ~

A Yorkshire man's dog dies and as it was a favourite pet he decides to have a gold statue made by a jeweller to remember the dog by.
Yorkshire man: "Can tha mek us a gold statue of yon dog?"
Jeweller: "Do you want it 18 carat?"
Yorkshire man: "No I want it chewin' a bone yer daft bugger!"

~ ~

Golf balls

A man got on a bus with both of his front trouser pockets full of golf balls and sat down next to a beautiful (you guessed it) blonde.

The puzzled blonde kept looking at him and his bulging pockets.
Finally, after many glances from her, he said, "It's golf balls."
The blonde continued to look at him for a very long time, thinking deeply about what he had said.
After several minutes, not being able to contain her curiosity any longer, she asked,
"Does it hurt as much as tennis elbow?"

The following is an extract from Percy's novel 'Politically Incorrect' which won Best Thriller at the Pinnacle awards.

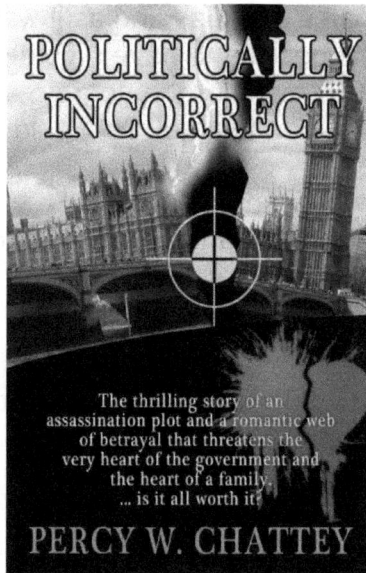

POLITICALLY INCORRECT

The thrilling story of an assassination plot and a romantic web of betrayal that threatens the very heart of the government and the heart of a family. ... is it all worth it?

PERCY W. CHATTEY

Pulling in the sheets, Paulo turned the vessel back on her original course, tightening the main sail as he did so. The jib, by now, was flapping, and he left it.

Sue saw the boat swing, and her heart sank as she realised the time had come for Paulo to change boats. She opened the throttles, and the twin engines started pushing the cruiser forward at a greater speed. The ride got ever rougher, and the noise as the waves broke across the craft frightened her.

She slowed the engines, afraid that the boat would break up if she continued to push it along at that increased speed. She noticed that the yacht was only under one sail and had slowed up dramatically. Slowly, but surely she started to make headway, the gap closing.

Paulo checked that the cruiser was catching up before going below to change into a rubber suit he had brought with him. On going down the companionway, the navigation table was on the right, and for the first time he noticed a ship's log book. It lay open, and unknown to him, the owner had put in the details of the voyage, including himself.

Holding on as the boat rocked and shuddered from the pounding waves, he picked up the book, flicking through the pages and noting how meticulously it had been kept. The whole history of the boat was there, ever since it had been purchased. Taking no chances, he threw the log book overboard.

It had become extremely cold, and as he stripped off his wet things, he shivered. He was not looking forward to the ordeal that lay ahead as he pulled on his wet suit.

By the time he had wiped the boat clean of fingerprints, just in case it was found in one piece, he was pleased to see "Zana 11" coming level with the stern of the yacht.

The waves were increasing in their ferocity, making it very difficult to stand on the deck. Sometimes the cruiser almost disappeared when the two boats were in troughs at the same time.

Susan was very worried. She could see her companion standing on the rear open deck of the sailing boat, but in the wildness of the wind and high seas it looked an impossible task to get a rope across to him so that she could pull him to safety.

They had gone over the theory of it many times, before he had left her but they had not reckoned on the weather being so bad. She tied a rope round her waist, firmly attaching it to a solid object but giving herself enough room for movement. She then started to edge the cruiser towards the other boat. Paulo had told her to come in from the leeward side as she would have more control over the boat, there was no telling what would happen when he left the other craft. The yacht could very easily swing round so it would be better if she approached so that no damage would be done, if that occurred.

Now she wondered on the wisdom of this, for she was finding it very difficult to avoid a collision. One or other of the boats would slide down the side of the wave in a spray of water, then the distance between them would become alarmingly close.

She waited, still edging the two boats closer together. She curled a rope ready to throw it, trying to work out a pattern of the craft as they came closer together, only to part again. She switched on the automatic pilot to keep "Zana II" on a straight course, then, opening the door, she stepped out on to the deck. The noise of the wind and the waves made communication between the two vessels impossible.

She waited, watching the two boats coming closer, as the waves pushed them side on. The gap was closing rapidly. She could feel the cold after the warmth of the cabin, her ears were stinging and she wished she had put a hat on. The boats were now rushing towards each other, and she held the rope, praying they would not collide. When she thought they were at the closest point, she threw the rope, lassoo style, towards her colleague. It caught the main sail, slipping to the deck about five feet from where Paulo was standing.

An Irishmen wanting to become a Priest and went to see the Bishop who said "You must answer 3 questions on the Bible"
"1st - Who was born in a stable?"
"Red Rum" he replied
"2nd - What do you think of Damascus ?"
"It kills 99% of all germs" he replied.
"3rd - What happened when the disciples went to Mount Olive ?"
"That's easy" he said "Popeye kicked the hell out of them!!"

My grandpa started walking
five miles a day when he was 60.
Now he's 97 years old and
we don't know where the heck he is.

A member of Parliament to Disraeli: *"Sir, you will either die on the gallows or of some unspeakable disease."*

"That depends, Sir, "said Disraeli, "whether I embrace your policies or your mistress"

~~~~~~

A woman asks a man who is travelling with six children, "Are all these kids yours?"
The man replies, "No, I work in a condom factory and these are customer complaints".

ATTORNEY: Doctor, before you performed the autopsy, did you check for a pulse?
WITNESS: No.
ATTORNEY: Did you check for blood pressure?
WITNESS: No.
ATTORNEY: Did you check for breathing?
WITNESS: No.
ATTORNEY: So, then it is possible that the patient was alive when you began the autopsy?
WITNESS: No.
ATTORNEY: How can you be so sure, Doctor?
WITNESS: Because his brain was sitting on my desk in a jar.
ATTORNEY: I see, but could the patient have still been alive, nevertheless?
WITNESS: Yes, it is possible that he could have been alive and is now practicing law.

My father taught me   TIME TRAVEL.
"If you don't straighten up, I'm going to knock you into the middle of next week!"

Warner Communications paid 28 million for the copyright to the song Happy Birthday, which was written in 1935!

The Fence Repair - Australian style !!!

Three contractors are bidding to fix a broken fence at Government House.

One is from Cabramatta, another is from Marrickville, and the third is from Lane Cove.

All three go with an official to examine the fence.

The Cabramatta contractor takes out a tape measure and does some measuring, then works some figures with a pencil.

"Well," he says, "I figure the job will run about $900, $400 for materials, $400 for my crew and $100 profit for me."

The Marrickville contractor also does some measuring and figuring, then says, "I can do this job for $700. That's $300 for materials, $300 for my crew and $100 profit for me."

The Lane Cove contractor doesn't measure or figure, but leans over to the government official and whispers,

"$2,700."

The official, incredulous, says, "You didn't even measure like the other guys. How did you come up with such a high figure?"

The Lane Cove contractor whispers back, "$1000 for me, $1000 for you, and we hire the guy from Marrickville to fix the fence."

"Done!" Replies the government official.

~~~~~~

Intelligent people have more zinc and copper in their hair.

The Carbon Paper Scam.

Now that we can talk to our banking facility every day even if it is only through a computer, at least it is possible to check your statement daily, which one should because if there is an error then you can normally put it right there and then.

Which leads on to a little story about fraud which at one time was quite rife way back in the days when secretaries and clerks used that clattering machine, the typewriter. It would be mostly women who would spend all of the working day punching out letters, but first they had to feed a sheet of paper into the carriage and normally two sheets of carbon paper to produce copies of the work. Let's take the Ford Motor Company, but then it could be any large organization. It does not take too much of an imagination to think of the masses of letters and the copies this company would produce every day, it must have run into the hundreds of thousands, letters to dealers and suppliers and of course customers.

Now some bright spark thought it was a good idea to send them an invoice for carbon paper and it became known as the 'Carbon Paper Scam'. It went on for a long time until auditors picked it up, for you see nobody ever checked the invoices, they just paid them, not realizing there was no order given for the stock and in fact there was no stock. It was reported the organizers of the scam got away with close on a million pounds, at that time it was an enormous amount.

I'll go back to bank statements and cannot help but feel that maybe some organizations are doing something similar to its customers. Let me explain. Three years ago we took out an agreement with a software company to pay them twenty three pounds per year on the due date of February.

Each year since then the payments have gone through as agreed. However this year they decided to take a second payment in May. If we did not check our bank statement every day, we would not have known about it and they would be that much richer and us that much poorer.

This is not the first time this has happened, on another occasion it was over one hundred pounds that had been wrongly debited. The point really is was it deliberate or just a computer hitch – either way it pays to check. Why daily you may ask, well if there is a debit that should not be there then you can stop it there and then, if you leave it to the next day it is too late the bank will have paid it. On one occasion we found a thousand pounds was missing but I think we would have noticed that anyway. I wonder how many people are paying a regular payment, which they know nothing about and should not be paying it. Take care!
www.percychatteybooks.com

~~~~~~

Dial Phone

Love old dial phones,
finger wheel appeal;
Prefer wondrous whirr,
special birr to monotony
of mobiles, cell phone
drone ... First romance
started from a call box,
last two pee never better
spent; moment eclipsed
by persistent pips.
Copyright Richard Seal 2016

The "F" word There are only 11 times in history where the has been considered acceptable for use.

They are as follows:

11. "What the @#$% do you mean, we are sinking?"
-- Capt. E.J. Smith of RMS Titanic, 1912

10. "What the @#$% was that?"-- Mayor Of Hiroshima, 1945

9. "Where did all those @#$%ing Indians come from?"-- George Custer, 1877

8. "Any @#$%ing idiot could understand that."
-- Albert Einstein, 1938

7. "It does so @#$%ing look like her!"
-- Picasso, 1926

6. "How the @#$% did you work that out?"
-- Pythagoras, 126 BC

5. "You want WHAT on the @#$%ing ceiling?"
-- Michelangelo, 1560

4. "Where the @#$% are we?"
-- Amelia Earhart, 1937

3. "Scattered @#$%ing showers, my ass!"
-- Noah, 4314 BC

2. "Aw c'mon Monica. Who the @#$% is going to find out?"
-- Bill Clinton, 1998

1. "There is no @#$%ing way Trump will ever become President"
-- Hilary Clinton 2016

The 'Middle Wife'
By an Anonymous 2nd grade Teacher

I've been teaching now for about fifteen years. I have two kids myself, but the best birth story I know is the one I saw in my own second grade classroom a few years back.

When I was a kid, I loved show-and-tell. So I always have a few sessions with my students. It helps them get over shyness and usually, show-and-tell is pretty tame. kids bring in pet turtles, model airplanes, pictures of fish they catch, stuff like that. And I never, ever place any boundaries or limitations on them. If they want to lug it in to school and talk about it, they're welcome.

Well, one day this little girl, Erica, a very bright, very outgoing kid, takes her turn and waddles up to the front of the class with a pillow stuffed under her sweater.

She holds up a snapshot of an infant. 'This is Luke, my baby brother, and I'm going to tell you about his birthday.'

'First, Mom and Dad made him as a symbol of their love, and then Dad put a seed in my Mom's stomach, and Luke grew in there. He ate for nine months through an umbrella cord.'

She's standing there with her hands on the pillow, and I'm trying not to laugh and wishing I had my camcorder with me. The kids are watching her in amazement.

'Then, about two Saturdays ago, my Mom starts going, 'Oh, Oh, Oh, Oh!' Erica puts a hand behind her back and groans. 'She walked around the house for, like an hour, 'Oh, oh, oh!' (Now this kid is doing a hysterical duck walk and groaning.)

'My Dad called the middle wife. She delivers babies, but she doesn't have a sign on the car like the Domino's man. They got my Mom to lie down in bed like this.' (Then Erica lies down with her back against the wall.) 'And then, pop! My Mom had this bag of water she kept in there in case he got thirsty, and it just blew up and spilled all over the bed, like psshhheew!' (This kid has her legs spread with her little hands miming water flowing away. It was too much!)

'Then the middle wife starts saying 'push, push,' and 'breathe, breathe.

They started counting, but never even got past ten. Then, all of a sudden, out comes my brother. He was covered in yucky stuff that they all said it was from Mom's play-center, so there must be a lot of toys inside there. When he got out, the middle wife spanked him for crawling up in there in the first place.' Then Erica stood up, took a big theatrical bow and returned to her seat.

I'm sure I applauded the loudest. Ever since then, when it's Show-and-tell day, I bring my camcorder, just in case another 'Middle Wife' comes along.

If you believe in the *Paranormal* then you will enjoy this true story which is repeated from Percy's novel
'Blitz & Pieces'

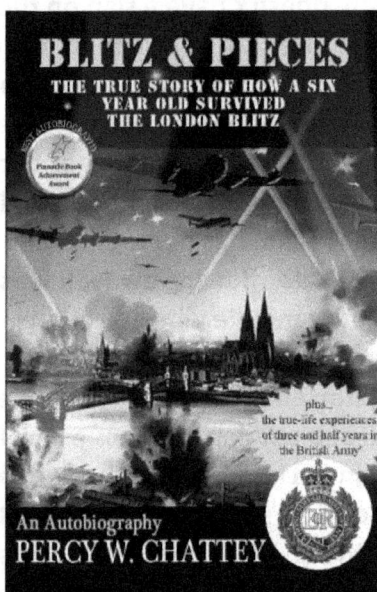

In the wilds of Exmoor in Devon there is a small hamlet called Challacombe, it consists of a few cottages, a quaint little inn, a phone box and a shop.

John Green the landlord of the inn, we had known for some time as he was the tenant in a hostelry in Mortehoe near Woolacombe in North Devon. His pub at that time was not far from where our caravan was sited, where we stayed for a break.

The following picture is the Ring O´ Bells and when it came on the market, John bought it, changed the name back to the original Black Venus, a reference to the ancient days when it was a hideout for smugglers. A problem he had in the bar was that you had to have your head bowed as the ceiling was very low, so he dug the dirt floor out and tiled it. As the ceiling was still not very high he hung thick leather straps from it like the ones in a railway carriage. It was strangely very comfortable hanging on one with a drink in the other hand while chatting.

In 1969 we took three months off from our business and stayed in Devon some of the time enjoying the delights of the tiny village. In the afternoon when the pub was closed we would go with John and our two children, to the beaches at Combe Martin.

John, always the joker, whose idea of breakfast was honey and cider! One day whilst sitting in the sun in a small cove, the tide started to turn and I knew that the beach would be covered in water and would block any path out of the area. John carried on dozing saying not to worry, when suddenly he jumped up dived into the water and disappeared. We were stranded the water had risen blocking the way out.

We stood looking around wondering what had happened to him. He had dived into the water and gone beneath the surface, and vanished, while the tide was still rising. The cliff behind us was tall and ragged with no paths. After about fifteen maybe twenty minutes of panic he came round the corner in a rowing boat. He had swum under the water around the corner of the cliff out of our sight, to get to the boat. He thought it was very funny I was not so happy, especially when he pushed me in complete with sports jacket and trousers, as I was sitting on the edge of the vessel, much to the delight of the children.

Once a fortnight I would drive back to London to attend to any outstanding business, it was on one of these trips on the 21st July 1969 that I watched the first Moon Landings on colour television in our lounge in Ley Street. Jean, who was still in Devon, could only watch it in black and white. Colour television only started broadcasting the year before initially in London. There were two television sets in our lounge one to watch pictures in black and white, the other for colour which only received programmes from BBC2 for a couple of hours a day.

In White Car days, our family and friends enjoyed the comfort and ancient décor with its timber beams of the Black Venus. I even treated my bank manager, Jimmy Rideout and a great friend solicitor Eddie to a long weekend there. We went horse riding one day and on another we walked across the moor, with steaks in the evening in the Inn's fine restaurant. Good for the soul and relaxation. And of course John a very good friend and fun to be with.

We had lost touch with John when he remarried a few years after the above events. By then we had moved to Bristol. I had a business appointment in Cornwall and had decided to drive down the previous evening. It was a dark moonless night and I was travelling on the A30 the other side of Okehampton on a pitch black empty road, and a little hungry with no eateries in sight. A little further on in the distance there were some lights which turned out to be a pub. I thought maybe they do food if not at least I will get a packet of crisps. I pulled into the almost deserted car park.

Behind the bar a tall sombre looking man dressed formally in black, a touch of old castles and Dracula came to mind. We instantly recognised that we knew one another. As the conversation progressed it turned out he used to be the landlord of The Queens, a pub in Ilfracombe in Devon. John and I had visited on a few occasions as he was a long- time friend of Johns and had also been his best man when he married his first wife.

I said something like I had not seen or been in touch with John for about twelve years. He replied, *"You don't know then?"* He paused looking at me and then said *"I have just come back from his funeral."* It turned out his liver finally gave up the fight.

What a coincidence to be on that road, which I rarely use, choose that pub on that particular night out of all the others on the two hundred mile journey to Cornwall. I left there slightly in shock and feeling a bit spooked.

Copyright www.percychatteybooks.com

If you have a similar spooky story to tell send it to percybooks@outlook.com, we will acknowledge receipt.

A bookseller conducting a market survey asked a woman,
"Which book has helped you most in your life?"
She replied, *"My husband's cheque book."*

****

A prospective husband in a book-store enquired,
"Do you have a book called, "Husband – the Master of the House"?
The sales-girl promptly replied, *"Yes sir, 'Fiction' and 'Humour' are on the 1st floor."*

The Pastor's Ass

Pastor entered his donkey in a race and it won.The Pastor was so pleased with the donkey that he entered it in the race again, and it won again.
The local paper read:

PASTOR'S ASS OUT FRONT.

The Bishop was so upset with this kind of publicity that he ordered the Pastor not to enter the donkey in another race..
 The next day, the local paper headline read:

BISHOP SCRATCHES PASTOR'S ASS.

This was too much for the Bishop, so he ordered the Pastor to get rid of the donkey..
The Pastor decided to give it to a Nun in a nearby Convent..
The local paper, hearing of the news, posted the following headline the next day:

NUN HAS BEST ASS IN TOWN.

The Bishop fainted!
He informed the Nun that she would have to get rid of the donkey, so she sold it to a farmer for $10.
The next day the papers read:

NUN SELLS ASS FOR $10.

This was too much for the Bishop, so he

ordered the nun to buy back the donkey and lead it to the plains where it could run wild. The next day the headlines read:

NUN ANNOUNCES HER ASS IS WILD AND FREE.

The Bishop was buried the next day

The moral of the story is...being concerned about public opinion can bring you much grief and misery. It can even shorten your life...So be yourself and enjoy life to the fullest.

~ ~

In 1847 during the Irish potato famine, the Choctaw Nation of Native Americans donated $147 to assist with famine relief. An Irish town built a memorial to thank Native Americans.

This is a lovely thought but I don't think so but if you know different then 'Story Telling' would like to hear from you at percybooks@outlook.com

WELCOME to 2017

```
Our Phones - Wireless...Cooking - Fireless
Cars - Keyless...Food - Fatless
Tires - Tubeless...Dress - Sleeveless
Youth - Jobless...Leaders - Shameless
Relationships - Meaningless
Attitudes - Careless...Babies - Fatherless
Feelings - Heartless
Education - Valueless
Children - Mannerless... Bills - Paperless
```

```
          We are-SPEECHLESS,
     Government-is CLUELESS,
     Politicians-are WORTHLESS!
```

Buried...THE STORY OF More NIGHTMARES!!!

Mike can feel himself slipping further and further down under the weight of a collapsing marriage, the spectre of impending redundancy, huge mortgage payments, the loan for his new car, and the kids' exorbitant school fees. Living well beyond his means has sunk him into a pit, he is slowly being buried alive. Each night, lying awake in bed for hours, Mike feels burned out, wanting to shout, surrounded by dark clay ...

In sleep, he becomes weightless, timeless, drifting through space; now displaced without form or sense of alarm, moving beyond calm into a realm lacking thought. Then dim figures from the past mutate, degenerate into shade-faded creatures of hate, bringing naked fright in the very deepest dead of night. A flesh tremor sent down his spine feels so intense whilst he is lying prone, without any form of defence.

Concealed behind the curtains or under the bed, lingers a sickening dread, a fear of death, nothingness and beyond. A slight figure appears nightly as a streak - A grime-grey shroud of cloud dissipating into a dirty stain. He asks himself in fleeting moments of consciousness if this shadow lady huddled in the corner, pulling at her long grey hair, imploring, trying to scream, rising to fall, is actually there at all.

As a small black cat sidles underneath his bed, the darkness gathers around cobwebs to form a tiny figure in a shapeless hat; she hovers above the stricken man awhile; she could be kindly with a half smile, but falters a moment in black, green to grisly mean. Puss emerges in the fading night - his enigmatic magic is, for now, dissipated by scant daylight.

Heavy rain and a loud branch crack end the nightmares, but not the interminable feeling of blackness. The morning returns him to the daytime show awhile - A range of roles to be performed with diligence, vigour; each of his faces are different, shifting, and always presented with a valiant smile. He knows only too well that the next night will attack, change tack, bringing many different realities back... Submerged, going under, soil sputtering in his mouth, heavy cold-sweating, limbs like led, he is yearning now for the last spadeful to be thrown over his head.

Copyright Richard Seal 2017

THE SECOND CHAPTER in Percy's new novel 'The Cormack's' Published August 2017

Gideon

Chapter Two

Gideon Cormack, a good looking boy in his earlier years, had never got over the trauma of being kidnapped from the boarding school where all of the family's children had been educated. The ruffians who had carried out the task had been employed to do so by others who had been determined, at the time, to convince the family to carry out an activity contrary to the Government laws. After the event and his return to his schooling he had restless nights with strong nightmares. The lack of sleep was also taking a toll on his studies, with the result he was receiving exceptionally poor marks.

He was also being tormented by his fellow pupils as they wanted to know what had taken place. On one occasion the group were sitting around a table all determined to hear what had happened to him during the period of his absence.

Originally the school's authority had been exceptionally firm in their instruction that he should be left alone to let the event and the experience of it, become a forgotten bad memory. However that was not to be as the men who had perpetrated the kidnapping were hauled before the courts and charged with the rape of the boy, amongst other actions.

The story was carried in the newspapers and Gideon's troubles came to the fore. His fellow pupils were determined to hear what had taken place, and after many jibes and hints he finally agreed to explain what had happened to him; in doing so he felt that the shock of it would be shared amongst friends, which would help to dissipate the disgust and the anguish of the sleepless nights, which hopefully would cease.

What he had not taken into account was that his class mates, although still boys, they were becoming young men with the sexual urges that accompanies that transition. They sat agog listening to his story, all leaning on the wooden table they were grouped around, as he explained in a faltering voice, the occurrence of being stripped naked and made helpless by being tied up over a bench while the men who had kidnapped him took it in turns to rape him.

Although he did feel better divesting himself of the happening after he had told them about his experiences, but he had not calculated their response. A few of his close friends were sympathetic whilst others wanted to know what it had felt like.

Suddenly he felt uncomfortable. How could he explain the embarrassment of it. In a school where the pupils shared the same showers and bathing area, being naked in front of others was not unusual and acceptable, but trying to explain what one felt like while being stripped naked by grown men who were exploring your body, was very different. It was then he realized that in some ways he had enjoyed it, and said so.

The others looked at him in shock, although there were some who smiled and were looking forward to chatting with him when they could get him alone. One of whom he felt an affinity for. It was as if they were the only two in the room. He could feel a change come over him and a tingle of excitement similar to what he had felt when he had been raped.

The meeting had broken up on the sound of the bell encouraging the pupils to return to their dormitories. They made their way in groups back to the night quarters talking about the story they had just heard. Gideon's schooling changed with regular liaisons in a dark room which he looked forward to. The original horror had dissipated and the close loving relationship with one of the other male pupils developed to his liking. He was disappointed when the time came to go out into the world, and by arrangement, when he finally left, he knew he would carry on seeing certain friends.

Sean, Gideon's father was proud of his son, but totally disappointed by his academic abilities after he had seen his school reports. Realising he was not ready to be part of the administration team, work was found for him around the factory which eventually developed into Gideon learning to drive. He became the principle person teaching others the skill of controlling a motor vehicle, at which he was very proficient.

Another disappointment came to his mother and father when he showed no interest in the fairer sex. The Annual Ball to be held at the Communal Rooms attached to the city hall was when the young ladies had finished their studies and were allowed to come out into the world.

Gideon, whilst his peers showed extreme excitement at the coming event, he could not join in their expectant pleasure as he had little interest in the female form as he had made up his mind to enjoy a different mode of pleasure. He had discovered there were drinking clubs where other males congregated in a secure sheltered place to practise their type of passion and it was where he became a regular visitor.

The clouds of war swept across Europe and the Dauntless Factory became a centre for excellence in producing vehicles for the Armed Forces Gideon became a useful member of the team organising the delivery of the various types of transport.

The Cormack family were proud of their status and the astuteness which had developed from their education and they looked on Gideon as the odd one out especially as he shunned female company. He was aware of this and became more and more secular in his ways and shunned mixing with family life. As a result he became an outcast and was treated with a certain amount of disdain.

When the Army called for volunteers, and very much to the family's relief to be rid of him, he joined the Royal Artillery where as the Principle Driving Instructor he taught the other soldiers to drive. It was a time when the Army was starting to realise the benefits of using motor transport as opposed to horse drawn vehicles to convey its troops and stores.

Nineteen sixteen arrived and Gideon was in his third year in the Forces, and as a non commissioned officer he arrived in France where he was part of a team delivering supplies to the front line. He had become an expert in handling the big wagons in off road conditions and had a reputation for being able to deliver to a destination, no matter how difficult the terrain was, where it had been mutilated by the constant shelling from either side.

It had been a strenuous period, with little rest he had been persistent in the assignment of making sure supplies continued to be delivered to the front line. As was normal in this difficult task, it was late afternoon when they set out, so when they neared their destination they would have the cover of darkness.

Gideon was driving the lead vehicle in a convoy of three with urgently needed stores and heading for a unit in the Ypres area where regularly the fighting had been the most violent. It had been five days since he had travelled this way and was surprised to see most of the road had been destroyed by shell fire in that period.

He was confident he was on the right road by familiar objects that had not been damaged, and remembered that when he got to a small village over the brow of a small hill, which was no more than a cluster of houses, he had to turn right.

It should not have come as a shock to him of a land devastated by constant shell fire to find the houses had almost been destroyed. To his horror the land mark he needed was totally different.

He stopped the small convey to get his bearings, as the road he required, and was vital to turn into was nonexistent with multiple craters covering the area. An explosion occurred to his left rocking the vehicle, which was followed by others some of which were very close. Checking the mirrors to see if the followers had not been hit by the constant falling military hardware exploding around them, he put the lorry into gear and chose what he thought was the right direction.

He was well aware that if they got into range of the enemy guns he would be the first they would fire at, and with the recent explosion so near to them he knew he must be in range of their big guns.

The day had started with a constant down pouring of rain and with great effort in the open cab of the lorry, he was cold and tired from struggling to keep the vehicle moving. The fire power from the opposing side was more fierce than normal and the shells were exploding nearby throwing stones and dirt over the Army convoy.

Although having difficulty in seeing he continued pushing forward. The landscape had changed from a week ago when he had last come this way, torn apart by the constant explosions. He wiped the water off the compass to check his direction. His heart sank as he saw he was going in North East direction when it should have been East.

He now knew for certain that he had gone wrong. He did not recognise the landscape around him, and was positive he was in the wrong direction to where he was supposed to be heading. When a machine gun opened fire with the bullets causing small explosions in a line on the ground immediately in front of him he knew he was very close to the enemy lines, and he shouldn't be.

He quickly swung the steering wheel to turn the lorry in a different direction. With his restricted vision he did not see the shell hole and the two front wheels of the Dauntless truck he was driving dropped into it. He was thrown forward and when the vehicle stopped it was nose down in the considerable sized crater. He looked behind him and saw that the lorry immediately behind him had taken a direct hit and was lying on its side with orange and black flames licking at the body work.

He climbed out from behind the steering wheel, feeling the hurt where he had fallen against it, and dropped into the dirty muddy waterlogged hollow where he lay against the side getting his breath. After a while, and with difficulty, he managed to ascend out of the hole, sliding and finding little grip on the sides which were nothing but slippery thick mud soaking wet from the rain.

Gideon managed to get to his feet and he was inspecting the lorry when the machine gun opened up again, the shells from it ploughing a furrow across the ground culminating in the lower part of his legs.

It took just over three weeks for Gideon to be transported back to England where he was hospitalised in the family's old home Tullamore, which had been turned into a hospital for the duration of the war. It was too late to save his legs as gangrene had set in and they had to operate and remove them from below the knee. The family's attitude changed towards him and now he was treated as a hero and was welcomed into their fold.

- -

Counsellor

Having filled his water jug and opened a new box of tissues, the Counsellor smiles warmly as he opens the door to his next client.

The young lady flounders in a fast-flowing stream of consciousness; as her tears fall freely, make-up rivulets criss-cross flushed cheeks. The Counsellor travels with his client without judgement for fifty minutes. As he gently leaves her journey, he helps her to collect herself with an offer of a tissue.

Next is a reluctant male, sent by his wife, who knows that 'seeing a shrink' will be a waste of time. He is happy about a shift to football talk, rapport secured through scores recalled, players related. As the Counsellor carefully asks about the man's thoughts, his defences erode; removing his jacket, he loosens, sits back and looks forward to the next session. He might have strayed offside, but the goal was given.

The third client looks through the Counsellor blankly. His words spoken softly hang a moment, before sinking in the silence. Her face, filling with lines, collapses, her fading words tumble mumble before a wail cuts a heart-soul fissure. Holding her pain, the Counsellor finds sobbing subsides slowly to calm. As the session ends, a small smile lifts to eyes slightly lighter. Her nose having been blown, control is re-claimed with her handbag clutched. She leaves, never to return.

Now alone, the Counsellor sits quietly for a few minutes, hand lightly rubbing his forehead before he resurfaces with a fresh face, returning to the room.

Copyright Richard Seal 2017

Shipping is cheap. So cheap that, rather than fillet its own fish, it is cheaper for Scotland to send its cod 10,000 miles over to China to be filleted and returned to Scotland.

The words 'racecar,' 'kayak' , and 'level' are the same whether they are read left to right or right to left (palindromes).

Why I Mow My Own Lawn
(A true story; you just gotta love Lee!)

One day, shortly after joining the PGA tour in 1965, Lee Trevino, a top professional golfer and married man, was at his home in Dallas, Texas , mowing his front lawn, as he always did.

A rather attractive lady driving by in a shiny Cadillac stopped in front of his house, lowered the window and asked, "Excuse me, do you speak English?"

Lee responded, "Yes Ma'am, I do."

The lady then asked, "What do you charge to do yard work?"

Lee said, "Well, the woman in this house lets me sleep with her."

The lady hurriedly put the car into gear and sped off!....

~ ~

TYPEWRITER is the longest word that can be made using the letters only on one row of the keyboard.

~ ~

The average person's left hand does 56% of the typing.

~ ~

The winter of 1932 was so cold that Niagara Falls froze completely solid.

Mathematics: Brilliant

This comes from 2 math teachers with a combined total of 70 yrs. experience.

What Makes 100%?

What does it mean to give MORE than 100%?

Ever wonder about those people who say they are giving more than 100%? We have all been to those meetings where someone wants you to give over 100%.

How about achieving 103%?

What makes up 100% in life?

Here's a little mathematical formula that might help you answer these questions:

If:

A B C D E F G H I J K L M N O P Q R S T U V W X Y Z

Is represented as:

1 2 3 4 5 6 7 8 9 10 11 12 13 14 15 16 17 18 19 20 21 22 23 24 25 26.

Then:

H-A-R-D-W-O-R-K

8+1+18+4+23+15+18+11 = **98% And**

K-N-O-W-L-E-D-G-E

11+14+15+23+12+5+4+7+5 = **96% But ,**

A-T-T-I-T-U-D-E

1+20+20+9+20+21+4+5 = **100%**

And,

B-U-L-L-S-H-I-T

2+21+12+12+19+8+9+20 = **103%** and

A-S-S-K-I-S-S-I-N-G will take to

1+19+19+11+9+19+19+9+14+7 = **118%**

So, one can conclude with mathematical certainty, that while:

Hardwork and **Knowledge will get you close, and Attitude will get you there.**

It's the Bulls**t and **Ass Kissing** that will put you over the top.

Now you know why Politicians are where they are!
I've never seen a better explanation than this formula. How true it is.

~ ~

ATTORNEY: How old is your son, the one living with you?
WITNESS: Thirty-eight or thirty-five, I can't remember which. ATTORNEY: How long has he lived with you?
WITNESS: Forty-five years.

The Chief Translator for the European Parliament can speak 32 different languages fluently

Another profound story from one of our favourite writers.

Two Biros

John Shilton was always well prepared for the next day's classes. His plastic box was sorted nightly, filled with resources to meet his students' needs and to cover all eventualities. He always liked to be equipped with two biros, purple or green, for marking (a spare of course, just in case). On this particular Friday, the new student teacher, Sally, was covering his morning classes, then he was due to have a lesson observation, which filled him with feelings of both excitement and foreboding.

Miss Peakman ('Do not let them call you Sally') frequently flushed, feeling crushed under the barrage of voices. Aware of faltering poise, she felt creeping sweating wetting the new shirt over her ruckled skirt. In a moment of white noise, she caught one lad's eyes - flecked black specks - whilst cheek was being shot. However, she smiled at the children so happy to be pushing boundaries and buttons, laughing at her lacking; How could they know Miss embraces the buzz of the job she loves?

Jane had had a long day. It was tough enough most days working as a Teaching Assistant in Shilts's classes without being thrown to the lions with that student woman. She had struggled to be her usual happy-clappy self when that little horror Mikey started kicking off. Good cheer had withered and frayed, Her teeth were sore from gritting and she had bitten her lip to bleeding again. She felt glad to mount her bike and take her feelings out on the road with some vigorous pedal pumping.

When his observer had arrived in the final lesson, John's stomach skip tripped, flip dipping for a moment. Minutes later, energised, he found the frowning woman had been disguised as furniture - clipboard unseen behind a mental screen. Stepping forward, he soared into his prime. The curtain had gone up - it was Showtime! However, there had been no space on his lesson plan for a seizure; The chest clutching collapse was unscheduled, improvised, the senior teacher's death leaving all surprised.

Copyright Richard Seal 2017

Frustration! Is trying to find your glasses without your glasses

A POEM to which anyone under forty can relate to.

I remember the corned beef of my Childhood,
And the bread that we cut with a knife,
When the Children helped with the housework,
And the men went to work not the wife.

The cheese never needed a fridge,
And the bread was so crusty and hot,
The Children were seldom unhappy,
And the Wife was content with her lot.

I remember the milk from the bottle,
With the yummy cream on the top,
Our dinner came hot from the oven,
And not from a freezer; or shop.

The kids were a lot more contented,
They didn't need money for kicks,
Just a game with their friends in the road,
And sometimes the Saturday flicks.

I remember the shop on the corner,
Where biscuits for pennies were sold
Do you think I'm a bit too nostalgic?
Or is it....I'm just getting Old?

Bathing was done in a wash tub,
With plenty of rich foamy suds
But the ironing seemed never ending
As Mum pressed everyone's 'duds'.

I remember the slap on my backside,
And the taste of soap if I swore
Anorexia and diets weren't heard of
And we hadn't much choice what we wore.

Do you think that bruised our ego?
Or our initiative was destroyed?
We ate what was put on the table
And I think life was better enjoyed.
Anon

Another teaser from Percy's new novel 'The Cormack's Published in July and available through most outlets.

Elisabeth

Chapter Seven

As was the custom in the Cormack's Organisation the Chief Executive of any of the Companies was a family member. Elisabeth had not been the first choice as the custodian of the Casino, when it was first being remodelled from the old Music Hall, in the early part of the nineteen hundreds. That had been Sir Roberts's sister Margaret, who had refused in horror, at the thought of running an establishment, which not only encouraged gambling but also pampered to the desires of the male population.

Mabel Fisher Cormack, a feisty lady who had strong thoughts about the male population, had been another choice, complying with the Cormack's unwritten rule of not wanting to employ, in a senior position from outside the family. She fancied the idea and had considered it seriously, until discussing the idea over with her husband Thomas, who was adamant and flatly refused to allow his wife to be in charge of such an establishment.

However Elisabeth, whose mother had been the sister of Sir Roberts father, had no such qualms, and looked forward to the task of seeing men belittle themselves because of their sexual needs.

She had been madly in love and had married, nearly thirty years previously at a very young age, to a debonair Army Officer. He had been a lot older by nearly ten years but that had not mattered to her at the time. He flattered her with his knowledge and money, and made her feel good.

One evening he had been daring enough to try and lift her skirts, which she had not experienced before and had pushed him away.

He was not going to be put off as he was infatuated with her and finally begged her to marry him. Because of the age difference the family were devastated, however Elisabeth had wanted him and got her own way.

She had been very happy and settled down to married life and adored the man she lived with and the attention he gave her.

It had been eighteen months after their wedding day when he told her he had been ordered to go to India to join his Regiment there.

For weeks she had been depressed about the news of him going, and despite the party held for him the day before he was due to leave, Elisabeth could not shake off the feeling of desperation at him going.

She had clung to him the evening before the soldier left knowing he would be away for a long time. The following day after his departure she was very distressed and almost mourned as if he were dead.

After a little while Elisabeth picked herself up and settled down to being a dutiful housewife, although still feeling and acting like a widow as she shunned any company, and looked forward to the time when he would return.

Her husband had been gone for over two months when more out of boredom than a need for more clothes, on a bright summer's day she decided to harness her pony and trap to go into the city of Liverpool. There were more outlets in the city to make a choice, as she fancied something bright and summery.

Out of decency and to stop any rumours of where she was going and what she was up to, a close neighbour accompanied her and they roamed around the various shops together, laughing and enjoying the day.

They had planned to have lunch at the Grand Hotel in the City Centre. They were totally relaxed and in a fine mood and especially pleased with the items they had purchased.

When they arrived at the plush foyer of the premises, both laughing with not a care to trouble them. A member of the hotel staff positioned at the main entrance, smartly attired in a burgundy uniform, greeted them and escorted them into the Restaurant and introduced them to the Maître de.

The two were happily chatting as they followed him to be shown to a table. The room was busy with people going to and fro, Elisabeth looked around the beautiful room, the glass chandeliers hanging from the ceiling casting a bright light around the large space, whilst still smiling and joining in with the chatter of her friend.

For Elisabeth it was like a fantasy, for in the far corner from where they were seated, an Army Officer in full uniform sitting with a lady friend.

She froze and held her hand up to her mouth and almost screamed. Her companion's eyes followed where she was looking, and quickly realised why her colleague and gone so pale, she held her hand out and touched her arm in reassurance.

Elisabeth turned away in shock. Suddenly she stood up and quickly returned to the foyer where she sat down heavily on a settee. Her companion who had followed joined her on the adjoining seat saying "That Army officer on a side table to the rear, was that your husband with another woman?"

She nodded her head. She got up slowly and went back to the opening to confirm to herself it was him. She wanted to go in and confront him, but knew in her heart he would only dominate her into believing something else, so she did nothing and walked away.

Her whole life had collapsed around her. The following months were hell and she had difficulty getting out of bed in the morning, and when she did manage to, nothing mattered and all she wanted to do was hide.

The hurt in Elisabeth was total. He had said he was going to India and now she realised that had been a lie to deceive her so he could be with this other person. Elisabeth made up her mind never to see him again, and she would never get involved with another man, and certainly not in a loving relationship.

It was a few months after the event at the restaurant when she received an invitation to attend a going away ceremony as her husband's Regiment was being transferred to India in the Far East. She was horrified at the thought of going as she had not heard from him since he had left home to go, as he said to India, and now she had the confirmation he had never gone.

Elisabeth was in a quandary about attending and decided not to. Six agonising months were to pass before some relief came to her by the way of a letter from the War Office, saying he had been killed in action while on active service. Eventually his personal things arrived, which, without seeing what the package contained, as the thought of opening it made her feel ill, she had it destroyed.

Once more she promised herself she would never trust or be involved with another man. That is until one day she met her friend Benet, the preacher. He was a kind man who treated her with respect and with no sexual desire. They found tender comfort in being together and, as she saw it, someone to hold her arm when they went to the theatre or elsewhere. Her personal desires could be satisfied whenever she wished with whoever she fancied. So when the family approached her to run the Casino, Elisabeth accepted it with open arms.

Author, Unknown...
Trapped Texas ATM repairman slips handwritten notes out of receipt slot pleading for help

A Texas repairman who became trapped inside an ATM slipped notes to customers via the receipt slot pleading for them to help him escape, police said. The contractor became stuck when he was changing a lock to a Bank of America room that leads to the back of the ATM, Corpus Christi police Lieutenant Chris Hooper said.

He could not let himself out of the room because he did not have a key card and the bank branch had been closed so there were no bank employees on site.

"Apparently he left his cellphone and the swipe card he needed to get out of the room outside in his truck," Lt Hooper said.

When he realised customers were withdrawing cash from the ATM, he passed notes to them through the receipt slot.

One read, "Please help. I'm stuck in here and I don't have my phone. Please call my boss ..."

Some customers appeared to dismiss the notes as a gag, Lieutenant Hooper said, but one called police.

"Sure enough, we can hear a little voice coming from the

machine," senior officer Richard Olden said.

"So we're all thinking this is a joke — this has got to be a joke."

After passing some shouts back and forth, an officer kicked in the door to the room and freed the man, whose name has not been released.

"Everyone is OK, but you will never see this in your life, that somebody was stuck in the ATM. It was just crazy," Mr Olden said.

- -

There are only four words in the English language which end in "dous": tremendous, horrendous, stupendous, and hazardous

- -

Wind

Living in the country, beauty,
peace, tranquility is unreal,
almost surreal for city folk ..
But nature, noticing a cozy
complacency creeping in
around vistas, then steps in
with wild winds whipped up
as if lost at sea, fit to shift,
lift fences, collapse a shed.
Likes to hurl tiles, cut power
to keep us all in our place ..
See if we still love the stars
with a tree lying on our car.
Copyright Richard Seal 2017

There are only two words in the English language that have all five vowels in order: "abstemious" and "facetious."

~ ~

Beautiful Game

Feels so amused watching 'The Beautiful Game'
reminding him still of a sole claim to fame.
At school he was always the last to be picked
for any sports team - he felt anxious and sick.

He finished in last place in each running race,
limped over the line so entirely shamefaced.
In a twelve man team he was always thirteen.
The teasing relentless, vindictive and mean.

Then one football team, so incredibly short
threw him into midfield to disgusted retorts.
Both sides were shocked seeing drama unfold:
He went on to score the game's solitary goal!

Copyright Richard Seal 2017

~ ~

When my boss asked me who is the stupid one, me or him? I told him everyone knows he doesn't hire stupid people.

This is a very interesting article and appreciation to Stuart for sending it to us.

Stuart Fisk Just because I'm #Brexit it does not make me a Fascist, Racist or Nationalist - I just want a Government to run a Country it's voted for, that we can have some control over at least - our system is not perfect, but that's why we have a vote, not an unelected body that does not voice or represent the concern of many of us... Reform comes within...

In 1973 the common market 'European Economic Market' was born (& I think this has been forgotten about) to enable free trade for common import on goods & it was a very very good idea in bringing Europe into trade with each other on an even keel, it was good & beneficial for all at that time and has been for many years.

However in recent years it has grown/morphed into something our Parents could never have imagined when they voted Yes some 43 years ago. Do you think they would have said Yes if they knew that where we are today is what they thought it would be yesterday?

We are a unique nation & slowly losing a voice of our own to Govern - I have no issues with anyone working anywhere in the world not just in Europe, to trade on equal terms. But that's all changed from its original concept & remit...

For me you should have some control on who comes in, similar to Australia, migration was plus 300K last year, we cannot sustain this...

Europe is broken, financial ruin in Greece, austerity everywhere else - it will not change, no matter how much you throw at it, Countries & people need to remember to live within their means.

There's no easy fix, but let us decide our own fate - Britain can work alongside the world once again, Governed by itself, working for itself.

We have immense Skill, Technology & the Passion to make it work - Don't let financial institutions scare us into believing we're doomed to fail or blackmailed by Europe & America into thinking we're not capable... We are 5th in the world in GPD, who needs who?

The UK contributes much more than it receives too, about €4.7bn more a year (now), but Europe says we gain more back in trade??? I can't see us losing that amount, as no one in Europe will suddenly stop trading with us.... will they...

To quote Churchill 'Solitary trees, if they grow at all, grow strong'

Strong we can be, strong we are already...
The Commonwealth works as a solid Union, trade as well as Strength, yet each country rules itself... That is how I see Britain working with Europe & the Rest of the World, as traders & friends, but able to Govern & decide what to do within its own borders, money & rules which fit purpose, which we able to disagree & vote on, we do not have that opportunity as it is, due to so many nations who disagree with us, is that European harmony?? NO...

Capitalism & Socialism can work when it speaks in the same voice - Britain had to give more money to Euro coffers because we did so well in GDP last year - imagine how many Doctors/nurses/police & health care workers that could pay for - new schools, social care for the elderly, infirm, those less fortunate, infrastructure (roads) & so on...

I've seen the severe cuts this country has had to endure and will continue to endure at first hand, those front line jobs could be saved if we diverted the money we raise within to those services mentioned.

We cannot fix the World, but if we make it on our own, which I have no doubt we can, the World will take note & drive them forward to succeed as well, thus creating a healthier World for all...

By all means go back to the original concept of the EEC for free trade, but not what it is today...

Amazing how many countries wanted their independence from Britain, but when we want our own Independence, everyone says no...

There is no perfect solution, but as a nation working together we can make it work...

Stuart Fisk

~ ~

Excerpt from Trudie Le Beau second novel
'White Gold'

CHAPTER 4

John, Lizzie and Eli sat huddled around the fireplace in the old parlour that they loved so much listening to the soft patter of rain on the windows as the wind blew it willfully and seemingly unceasingly at the sodden dwelling. Jess and Shiner were stretched out on a rug soaking up the heat from the open fire, snoring blissfully without a care in the world, as only dogs can do. It had been a hard winter, so far made worse by all the comings and goings of the tradesmen working on their new house. The constant traffic coupled with the sleet and snow over the last few weeks had churned up the ground around the house so that they were living in a sea of mud.

It had been almost eleven months now since Jake and India had set off for the south seas and, despite there having been a multitude of things to organise which had taken up a great deal of their time, all three missed the boys so much and all three could not help but worry for their safety, although none of them gave voice to their fears.

Lizzie was just about to suggest toasting some bread when the dogs jumped up and ran to the door, whining to be let out. A few seconds later they heard the jingling of a harness - the mud silencing any noise that may have been made by wheels or hooves.

Lizzie looked out exclaiming "Who on earth can that be on such a miserable day? Well now, it's one of the Villiers' carriages if you like! I don't know what they can be after but they'll not find a welcome here and that's for certain." She opened the door letting the dogs out and the rain in. Putting a hand up to shield her eyes she saw Alice's maid Sarah about to get down from the carriage but very uncertain as to how to avoid the mud. Lizzie called out "Wait Sarah. Stay there for a moment - what do you want?"

"Oh Miss Lizzie please can I come in? I just don't know what to do, and they want to take the baby away."

"What baby? What are you talking about? Just wait there and I'll get John to carry you in." She spoke to the driver. "You had better come in too poor man. It's not a day to be out in and no mistake."

Hearing some of the conversation curiosity got the better of John and Eli and they both appeared at the door. "John, poor Sarah seems to be in a fine old state. Can you put on your boots and fetch her in. I know I said no-one from the big house would be welcome here but Sarah is not one of them and she seems very troubled."

A few minutes later five people were sitting around the parlour table and two wet and muddy dogs were once again stretched out warming themselves. Sarah spoke "Thank you for fetching me in. I don't know what to do see. It's all so awful and there's no-one I know that can help 'cept maybe you."

John spoke "What is it child? Are you in some sort of trouble? What could you have done that would make you come here of all places?"

Sarah looked around, her eyes resting on Eli. "It's real private like. It's not me. It's Lord and Lady Villiers, and my poor Alice."

"Anything you have to say can be said in front of Eli, he is family and I would trust him with my life, but what about the young lad here?"

"Oh, Peter knows all and is as worried as I am. He was the one suggested we come to you for help. I just hope someone can do something."

"Right then Sarah, you had better start at the beginning while Lizzie fetches us all a drink - now what's all this about a baby."

"Oh, she is so sweet and so pretty, looks just like your Jake, and they want to send her away. My poor Alice is going mad with worry and..."

Lizzie dropped the tankard of ale she was about to hand to John. "Who looks just like Jake? Did you say a baby looks just like Jake?"

"Yes Miss Lizzie, and those horrible Shorcrosses want to send the poor little mite away - get rid of her."

Lizzie stood frozen to the spot but before she could speak John took over. "Like I said Sarah, start at the beginning - take your time and don't let yourself get upset. Off you go - we are all ears."

Martialling her thoughts, Sarah began. "Well, you know that

Jake wanted to marry Alice and my master would have none of it. I remember that day he was sent off with a flea in his ear 'acos the next day Lady Catherine she sent me here with food and that - d'you remember?" Everyone nodded. "Well, she give me two letters, one for India and one for Jake. I didn't know what was in them but she made me promise to give them both to India and not to tell no-one else about them. All I know is that Miss Alice was heartbroken when Jake left - heartbroken, and Lady Catherine and his Lordship weren't much better I can tell you. The worst thing was that Robert Shorcross was hanging around all the time, and the way he spoke to Lady Catherine and Sir Edward - well, none of us staff could believe it. We just couldn't understand why he wasn't sent packing. One day old Morton confronted him about speaking to the master in such a rude way and he did no more than strike him across the face and throw him out. So now we've got two new men who are loyal to Shorcross, and they are horrid, treat the rest of us like dirt don't they Peter?" Peter nodded his affirmation.

"But that is terrible. He has been at Fenton ever since I can remember. What happened to him?"

"They say he's in the village and really down on his luck, poor old boy - but that Shorcross wouldn't give tuppence about that.

John turned to Eli. "Maybe tomorrow you could try to find him, and if you do bring him back here? He's a good man and I'm sure we can find something for him to do. I'm beginning to really dislike this Robert Shorcross and what I can't understand is why on earth Villiers is putting up with such things, it makes no sense."

"Ah, well it does see 'acos when she found out that Lady Alice was going to have a baby Lady Catherine collapsed - she was quite poorly. Anyway, it was then she told me how they were being blackmailed 'acos years ago she had helped a friend of hers to escape after he shot Shorcross's Pa in a duel. This friend was wanted for murder see, so she would be in a lot of trouble if he told. She said Shorcross wanted to marry Alice and take half of their estate and if they didn't agree he would see that Lady Catherine went to prison, and now of course, on top of all that, he's threatening to shame Alice by telling everyone that her baby belongs to a farm hand!"

"He is insisting that little Elizabeth is given away as soon as they can find a wet nurse, and that he and Alice be married before the Summer is out. Them letters that Lady Catherine gave me were to explain all this to Jake. They had no choice but to send him away without telling him the truth see, 'acos they were frightened he would do something stupid and get himself into real trouble. She didn't know about little Elizabeth then of course."

At this point Sarah could not hold back more tears and struggled to carry on. "Like I said just now my poor Miss Alice is beside herself with grief - she's talking about running away but Lady Catherine would suffer for it, and anyway where would she go? It's all so awful. There is nothing but misery up at the house - nothing but misery. If I wasn't afraid of hanging I'd do for that Shorcross pig and no mistake."

Peter nodded, "Me too."

"So, what you are telling us is that Lizzie and I have a Granddaughter and unless Alice agrees to marry Shorcross and give the child away he will make sure that she is disgraced and her mother goes to prison?"

"That's about it Mr Faraday. No-one knows the whole story 'cept me and Peter, and Morton of course, and most people don't know about the baby yet. We want to help but don't know how. All I know is that Miss Alice is suffering so and I can't bear to see it much more." Sarah burst into tears once again and this time was unable to hold them back.

John, Lizzie and Eli sat in stunned silence.   Ever since Jake's departure they had held a grudge against the Villiers family, hating them for the cruel way they had rejected their son, and now they hear that all the while Shorcross had been holding them to ransom, feeding off them like some disgusting parasite.   John banged the table with his fist.   "We are beholden to you Sarah for coming to us, otherwise we would never know about the baby, or the trouble that your mistress is in.   Say nothing of this to anyone on your return.   We will call on his Lordship tomorrow and maybe think of a way to help.   Don't look so worried girl. I'm sure his Lordship will realise that you only have their best interests at heart, and at a time like this I'm sure he will welcome our support and friendship.   Now, before you both leave pull up your chairs and let's enjoy a plate of Lizzie's hotpot, you both look as though you could do with it."

The two loyal servants left Spinnaker feeling much better than when they had arrived.   All their anxieties about betraying secrets had been allayed by John's assurances of his discretion, and it had proved to be a real relief to have off loaded their worries.

When they had seen off the two young folk, John and Lizzie clung together.   They had a Granddaughter - Elizabeth.   They were elated but at the same time fearful of her safety - if only Jake were here.

Eli sat by the fire fondling Shiner's ear.   He thought about Robert Shorcross, a man he had never met, but he knew the type, oh yes he knew the type and he hated their ilk with every ounce of his being.

After very little sleep John and Lizzie were up at the crack of dawn anxious to visit Fenton Park, killing time with a few chores, waiting for a respectable time to call.   Nerves jangling like their horse's bridle they set off, not at all sure of the reception they would receive.

As it happened their misgivings had been ill founded and they were welcomed effusively by the Villiers. Both John and Lizzie were quite shocked at how much they had both aged. They had lost a considerable amount of weight and his Lordship had the look of a whipped dog. Making sure that all servants were out of earshot John got straight to the point, explaining that Sarah had told them everything and they had come to help in any way they could. A wave of relief washed over Catherine and Edward Villiers; they had lived in fear of anyone finding out their secrets and now here were Jake's parents, not only accepting of them, but offering help and the hand of friendship. Bolstered by this welcome turn of events Catherine summoned Sarah and sent her to fetch Alice and baby Elizabeth; all had gone well then.

Alice entered the drawing room tentatively not knowing what to expect from John and Lizzie after her father's rebuttal of Jake. She need not have worried. They both greeted her with open arms billing and cooing over the baby – their first Granddaughter.

Tea was sent for and the two sets of parents, Alice and Sarah gathered round in a council of war, they had to find a way to deal with Shorcross, to get rid of him once and for all. They were interrupted almost immediately when the man himself swept into the room. "I gave instructions that we were not to be disturbed. How dare you just waltz in here as though you own the place!"

"Temper; temper now Edward. I do own the house, or at least I will very shortly own half of it. What are these people doing here? Are they the only folks who will consort with you nowadays? I would like them to leave – now! And Alice take that brat out of my sight, she displeases me so."

John was outraged that someone could talk to his Lordship in such a way, and calling his Granddaughter a brat was more than he could take. "How dare you speak to these people so? You have no right here and never will, we'll see to that. Now get out before I am forced to throw you out. Go and find a stone to crawl under you..."

His words stung the spoiled egotistical and arrogant Shorcross and he strode across the room raising his riding crop aiming to strike John across the face. "Who do you think you are talking to man? I'll not take insults from a peasant such as you."

John strode to meet him, grabbing the hand with the whip with his left hand, delivering an uppercut to his opponent's jaw with his right, knocking him flat. Shorcross, a soft living self indulgent man running to fat was no match for John and lay fighting to contain the tears that were gathering behind his eyes. When he had regained some composure he pulled himself up to his feet and tried his best to hide his humiliation with a lop-sided sneer – made difficult by his fast swelling jaw.

"You will regret that Faraday. I'll make sure that you and that no-good son of yours pay for today for the rest of your miserable lives." He turned on his heel and left the room with as much dignity as he could muster.

Edward Villiers clapped his hands "Oh my dear chap. You have no idea how many times I have wanted to do that, but I have to consider my family."

His brow creased with worry, "You must be really careful now. That man is poison and I fear now that he will do his best to wreck your life – you can count on it."

"I know your lordship, but that snake has had you at his mercy for far too long and we've got to do something about it.   Is there anyone you can call on, anyone legal like that could help?"

Sir Edward sighed. "I'm afraid, John that all my so called friends seem to have deserted us.   Everyone knows that Shorcross has designs on Alice and he and his mother will stop at nothing to get what they want. Blackmail, murder, you name it. They have many powerful and influential friends, all of them corrupt, so everyone of any repute stays well clear of them, and now consequently me. I am very much afraid there is a paucity of good men and true making you my dear sir one of the very few. You can be assured that whatever becomes of our family Catherine and I will always be indebted to you for your offer of help in our hour of need. "

"Well then maybe I should travel up to see Giles Mason. He was a trusted friend of Lord Henry and remained true to him when he was in trouble, and according to Jake he is well worth his salt. Try to keep things ticking along here and stay out of that bastard's way and I'll leave for London the day after tomorrow."

Hot tea was sent for, then John and Lizzie made to take their leave but not before Lizzie had held the baby for a while. She sat gazing at the beautiful blonde haired, blue eyed child who reminded her so much of her dear son, *"Oh Jake hurry home. Alice needs you – we all need you."*

Eli was waiting to hear the news when the pair arrived home. John related it all clenching his fists when he spoke of the way the parasite that was Robert Shorcross was lauding over everyone. The news worried him. He knew that John had made a powerful enemy who would make it his business to crush him without compunction at the first possible opportunity, a dangerous enemy indeed!

The two men spent the next day consulting with builders, checking livestock and dealing with all the minutiae entailed in running the fast changing Spinnaker. They all had an early night so that John would be fresh for his travels the next day. He would ride into Poundsmill where he would get a lift to the nearest coaching house. At least now they didn't have to worry about paying for such things.

Sleep eluded Eli so in the end he gave up and, with Shiner at his heels strolled along the coastal path in the moonlight.   He thought back to the time when he and John had struggled along that path down to the bay where they had disposed of the bodies of Cyrus Mallet and Cooper.   He shuddered – now they were plagued by that bastard Shorcross – why were there so many evil men in the world?

John was up with the sun saddling up his new gelding Juno, eager to be on his way when three men rode into his yard. He recognized two of them as the new servants at Fenton House; the third was a severe looking weasel of a man who ignored John's greeting.

The latter spoke "John Faraday we have reason to believe that you have stolen items of silverware belonging to the Villiers Estate and I have here written authority to search your property for such goods.

"Who the heck are you and what on earth are you talking about? I've never stolen a thing in my life and what the hell would I want with silver?"

All three men dismounted, and the two servants were directed to begin searching the barn and outhouses whilst their sour faced leader thrust some sort of document at John's chest. "Read this. You will see it is all above board. I am the new magistrate, here to do my duty."

Having heard raised voices Eli came into the yard. "What's up John? What are these folks doing here so early of a morning?"

"They are saying I stole some silverware from the Villier's place! I've never heard anything so damned stupid in all my life." Angrily he turned to the magistrate. "I've had enough of this. How dare you come here accusing me! Get off my land – NOW."

He was just about to manhandle this unwelcome little upstart onto his horse when. "Found it." Grinning from ear to ear both men came out from the barn, one of them holding a sack. He jiggled it up and down causing the contents to jangle. He peered inside the sack then pulled out a silver salver, holding it up for all to see. "There's a lot more in here. We got him red- handed. He can't deny he's a thief now."

Lizzie came out. "John, Eli, what's going on. Who are these men?"

John was speechless. Eli spoke "They're Shorcross lackeys accusing John of stealing silverware from his Lordship. They all know he's done no such thing – they knew exactly where to look for it because they put it there themselves."

"How dare you sir." The magistrate turned to John. "John Faraday you will come with us, along with the evidence of your crime and if his Lordship wishes it you will be transferred to a place of correction until such time as your trial takes place."

Lizzie screamed "No!"

John tried to reassure her. "It's alright Lizzie. This is nonsense and as soon as I speak to Sir Edward all will be well."

"Look after things here Eli. I'll be back soon."

With a sinking heart Eli watched them go. He knew of course Robert Shorcross was responsible for this and although he could not confide it to Lizzie, he feared that he would never see his dear friend again.

John was fuming. He knew that his Lordship would never stoop to such a level. No, it was Shorcross for sure, paying him back for boxing his ears. Well just wait until he gets to Fenton House – he'd give the sniveling snake another hiding.

As they approached the fork in the road that led to the Villiers Estate, John saw a waiting carriage and was suddenly afraid; he knew then there was treachery at hand, that he would likely be punished for these trumped up charges and no-one would know where he was.

Eli and Lizzie started at every sound for the rest of the day but by nightfall they had both accepted that John would not be returning home. Unable to concentrate on anything other than John's fate, they hitched up their pony and trap at first light and drove to Fenton House.

They were greeted by Lady Catherine who welcomed them in, curious as to what they might want so early in the day. When they explained the reason for calling she rushed off into the library calling out to her husband. They both returned ashen faced; it was obvious that they knew nothing about John's arrest or indeed that any of their silver was missing.

Shorcross it seemed had left for London the previous day, leaving his men to do his dirty work. Lizzie began to sob. They had no idea where John was or what was going to happen to him. Eli's heart turned to steel. He resolved there and then to do all he could to find and help his friend and to make Shorcross pay, with his life if necessary.

~ ~

The Architectural Designer.

Near to the centre of Bristol on a corner in Stokes Croft, I was called to a tall three storey empty dilapidated building built at the end of the eighteen hundreds. I had been approached by the new owners who wanted to turn it into flats on the top floor. In the vast open ground floor was to be a restaurant, with below in the large cellar a night club.

After a long discussion involving the Local Authority the idea of having flats was discarded, as the problem of creating separate safe exit from the top floor coupled with how to stop the transmission of noise between the flats and from activities on the lower floors, made it a non starter.

The Ground floor restaurant was straight forward as a design project, but as was normal when working out chair and table space, the client always wanted more than what was possible in the available area. We finally settled on an acceptable layout.

The Cellar had different problems. It was unusual in that it had plenty of head room and it was large in floor space. However, there were two entry points and while suitable as they were at opposite ends, their size was not adequate, as they were too narrow.

There was another serious problem the structure had unusually large girders supporting the ground floor, these had to be large as there were no supporting columns to the centre. These Steels were two and half metres apart and stretched from side to side.

After carrying out the survey, it became clear it was going to be difficult to fit in a staircase to comply with Building Regulations. If the exit stairway was straight, with no turns, then because of the closeness of the girders, which were at right angles to it, we could not comply with the height requirement over the steps. And it was not possible to cut the steels.

According to regulations, because of the available floor space there had to be two exits each a minimum of 1.5 metres wide. After juggling with the floor space by increasing the size of the toilet facilities, therefore reducing the night club space which in turn reduced the amount of guests, we received agreement from the Building Inspector that he would accept the rear exit as being one metre wide, which it was, providing the other one was two metres in width.

After more juggling on the drawing board with heights and widths, I eventually solved the puzzle by turning the stairway to fit in between the two and a half metre width of the steel beams, going up to a landing and then a right turn to the exit, we could make it fit. I marked the drawings very clearly that there must not be any deviation of the dimensions as shown.

In the regulations each step has to be exactly the same size and also the uppers, not one in the whole run can be different. So it was with surprise that some time later the builder telephoned to say the staircase did not fit and could he make the last top step shorter as he was 30mm undersized.

In panic I went to the site certain in my mind it should have fitted and wondering what, if anything I had missed out.

The builder had a long face when I arrived. He had started the staircase at the bottom and in a timber construction worked his way up. We studied the 'blue Prints' which I had designed. With a tape we started to check measurements. At floor level where the side of staircase as constructed should have been, it was 30mm further away from the wall as shown on the drawing.

I looked at him and grinned telling him that was his problem.
Copyright 2017 Percy W. Chattey

Thank you for reading and we hope you have enjoyed

'Story Telling Four'

Number 'Five' will be out in three months time with more short stories rhymes and some would say nonsense.

www.percychatteybooks.com

www.ingramcontent.com/pod-product-compliance
Lightning Source LLC
Chambersburg PA
CBHW060521030426
42337CB00015B/1958